W0357424

Zentralabitur 2011
Originalprüfungen
Englisch
Gymnasium/Gesamtschule

Autorin:
Eva-Maria Knocke (Lösungsvorschläge Originalprüfungen)

NORDRHEIN-WESTFALEN

ZENTRALABITUR **2011**

Originalprüfungen

ENGLISCH

Prüfungsaufgaben mit Lösungen
Leistungskurs

GYMNASIUM/GESAMTSCHULE

Cornelsen

Die in diesem Werk angegebenen Internetadressen haben wir überprüft (Redaktionsschluss 01.07.2010). Dennoch können wir nicht ausschließen, dass unter einer solchen Adresse inzwischen ein ganz anderer Inhalt angeboten wird.
Nicht in allen Fällen war es uns möglich, den Rechteinhaber ausfindig zu machen. Berechtigte Ansprüche werden selbstverständlich im Rahmen der üblichen Vereinbarungen abgegolten. Wir bitten um Verständnis.

www.cornelsen.de

Bibliografische Information: Die Deutsche Bibliothek verzeichnet diese Publikation in der Deutschen Nationalbibliografie; detaillierte bibliografische Daten sind im Internet über http://dnb.ddb.de abrufbar.

Projektleitung: Uta Kural, Cornelsen Scriptor Berlin
Redaktion: Anke Simon, Siegen
Gesamtgestaltung: Beate Schubert u. Uta Eickworth, Berlin
Gesamtherstellung: Dagmar & Torsten Lemme, Berlin
Satz/Layout: Dagmar & Torsten Lemme, Berlin
Umschlagentwurf: Patricia Müller, Berlin
Druck und Bindearbeiten: CPI - Clausen & Bosse, Leck
Printed in Germany
ISBN 978-3-06-150060-3

Gedruckt auf säurefreiem Papier,
umweltschonend hergestellt aus chlorfrei gebleichten Faserstoffen.

Inhaltsverzeichnis

LÖSUNGSVORSCHLAG 2009

PRÜFUNGSAUFGABEN 2010

LÖSUNGSVORSCHLAG 2010

Seiten (OP/L)	Texte	Aufgabentyp	Thema
	Literarische Texte		
18/24	Manil Suri: The Death of Vishnu	Comprehension, analysis, evaluation	The post-colonial exper in India The role of the New Eng literatures: Indian and Pakistani communities i Britain
44/50	Joyce Carol Oates: Dreaming America	Comprehension, analysis, evaluation	The American Dream th and now Economic and ecologic issues
70/76	Edward Albee: Who's Afraid of Virginia Wolf?	Comprehension, analysis, evaluation	Science and ethics: ger engineering
	Sachtexte		
21/34	Tony Blair's Lord Mayor's Banquet Speech	Comprehension, analysis, evaluation	Economic and ecologic issues International peace-keeping at the tu the century: the role of UN and the USA The post-colonial exper in India
47/61	Heather Brooke: Has anybody in Britain actually read '1984'?	Comprehension, analysis, evaluation	British history: modern democracy International peace-kee at the turn of the centu the role of the UN and t USA
73/86	Brandon Robshaw: Why it's time to give the Bard the heave ho!	Comprehension, analysis, evaluation	Shakespeare and the Elizabethan World In-depth study of a play corresponding film pass ges/scenes from theat performances

Für Schnelle:
Sie müssen mindestens 1 Originalprüfung mit Lösungsvorschlägen pro Textsorte gelesen haben.

r	Original-prüfung	Lösung	bearbeitet/ gelesen am			Kommentar
)8						
)9						
0						
)8						
)9						
0						

Für Gründliche:
Sie sollten mindestens 1 Originalprüfung pro Textsorte gelesen und gelöst haben.

Liebe Abiturientin, lieber Abiturient!

Im Frühjahr ist es so weit: Sie werden Ihre Abiturprüfung ablegen! Dieses Buch hilft Ihnen, sich effektiv auf den schriftlichen Prüfungsteil vorzubereiten.
Wir haben es so aufgebaut und geschrieben, dass Sie selbstständig damit arbeiten können. Das Buch enthält die zentral gestellten Originalprüfungen der letzten Jahre aus Ihrem Bundesland. Sie können also die typischen Aufgabenarten kennenlernen und üben. Auf diese Weise bereiten Sie sich ganz gezielt auf Ihre Abiturprüfung vor!

Wie sind die **Originalprüfungen** aufgebaut?

Hinweise zu den Prüfungsbestimmungen: Hier findet man in Kürze alle wichtigen Informationen rund um die Prüfung: den Ablauf, die Prüfungsteile usw.
Originalprüfungen und Lösungsvorschläge: Diese sind nach Jahrgängen sortiert. Man findet abwechselnd immer zuerst die zentral gestellten Originalprüfungen des Kultusministeriums und dann die Lösungsvorschläge, die wir für Sie erarbeitet haben.

Was ist das Besondere an diesem Buch?

Die **Originalprüfungen** lassen sich dosieren: für Schnelle und für Gründliche.
Für Schnelle: Wenn Sie schnell einen Überblick brauchen, lesen Sie erst die Prüfungen, notieren einige Lösungsansätze und vergleichen sie dann mit den Lösungsvorschlägen. Natürlich ist hier der Übungseffekt geringer.
Für Gründliche: Wenn Sie sich intensiver vorbereiten wollen, lesen Sie die Prüfungen und versuchen Sie, diese vollständig zu lösen. Bei Schwierigkeiten helfen die Lösungshinweise und Tipps. Erst zum Schluss vergleichen Sie Ihre Lösung mit der im Buch. Denken Sie daran, den Schnell-Check am Ende ehrlich auszufüllen. Dann sehen Sie, wo noch Übungsbedarf besteht.

	OP lesen	Lösung lesen	OP selbst lösen	Tipps nutzen und Lösungen vergleichen
Zeitfaktor	👍	👍👍	👍👍👍	👍👍👍👍
Lernfaktor	👍	👍👍	👍👍👍	👍👍👍👍
Prüfungserfolg	👍👍	👍👍👍👍	👍👍👍👍👍👍	👍👍👍👍👍👍👍👍

Klar ist: Je gründlicher Sie sich vorbereiten, umso besser werden Sie beim Abitur abschneiden!

Was ist das Besondere an den Lösungsvorschlägen?

Für dieses Buch haben erfahrene Lehrerinnen und Lehrer extra leicht verständliche und gut gegliederte Lösungen zu den Originalprüfungen geschrieben. In den Lösungsvorschlägen finden Sie auch viele **Tipps** und **Hinweise**, die die beste Herangehensweise erklären und Ihnen in der Abiturprüfung helfen werden.

Wie finde ich mich in den Originalprüfungen zurecht?

Eine gute Orientierung ist das **Inhaltsverzeichnis**, in dem man schnell die gewünschten Jahrgänge und Teilbereiche der Prüfungen findet.
In der **Übersicht** auf der vorigen Doppelseite können Sie gezielt nach bestimmten Themen und Aufgabentypen suchen.
Die **Kopfzeile** ganz oben im Buch lässt sofort erkennen, in welchem Prüfungsjahrgang man ist. Außerdem sehen Sie, ob Sie sich in den Prüfungen oder in den Lösungsvorschlägen befinden - und in welchem Teilbereich/welcher Aufgabe.
Weiterhin findet man vor jeder Aufgabe eine Mini-Tabelle. Dieser können Sie auf einen Blick wichtige Informationen zu der folgenden Prüfungsaufgabe entnehmen (z. B. zum Thema oder dem Aufgabentyp).

Woher weiß ich, ob ich schon gut vorbereitet bin?

Die **Schnell-Checks** helfen Ihnen, Ihre Fähigkeiten selbst einzuschätzen. Sie finden sie immer am Ende der Lösungsvorschläge. Seien Sie hier ehrlich zu sich und markieren Sie, wie Sie abgeschnitten haben.
Bei sollten Sie natürlich weiterüben. Tipps, die beim Weiterüben helfen, haben wir gleich dazugeschrieben.

Mit welchen Büchern kann ich noch üben?

Da das Abitur Ihre bisher wichtigste Prüfung ist, wollen Sie sich vielleicht noch intensiver vorbereiten. Mit **Abitur-Training** und **Abitur-Wissen** erhalten Sie noch mehr Material zum Üben und Wiederholen - so können Sie Ihrem Wunschprüfungsergebnis näher kommen.

Viel Erfolg!

Hinweise zu den Prüfungsbestimmungen

Wie läuft die Prüfung ab?

Die Aufgaben zur Prüfung werden zentral gestellt und finden an allen Schulen in Nordrhein-Westfalen, an denen Abiturprüfungen durchgeführt werden, am gleichen Tag statt.
In Englisch können die Schülerinnen und Schüler zwischen zwei Abiturvorschlägen wählen. Die Auswahlzeit beträgt 30 Minuten. Die Prüflinge dürfen nur einen Vorschlag bearbeiten. Falls jemand beide Vorschläge bearbeitet, kann nur eine Klausur gewertet werden, selbst wenn beide Vorschläge komplett gelöst wurden. Inhaltlich beziehen sich die Prüfungsvorschläge auf die in der Qualifikationsphase bearbeiteten Schwerpunktthemen.
Während der Klausur sind – wie bei den Klausuren in der Qualifikationsphase – ununterbrochen Lehrkräfte als Aufsicht anwesend. Ein Gang zur Toilette ist selbstverständlich möglich, jedoch kann jeweils nur ein Schüler bzw. eine Schülerin den Raum verlassen.

Wie lange dauert die Prüfung und welche Hilfsmittel sind erlaubt?

Die Prüfung im LK Englisch dauert inklusive der 30-minütigen Auswahlzeit 285 Minuten.
Im Allgemeinen stellt die Schule sowohl ein- als auch zweisprachige Wörterbücher zur Verfügung. Es besteht theoretisch die Möglichkeit, dass die Prüflinge eigene Wörterbücher mitbringen. Voraussetzung dafür ist, dass der Umfang ca. 150 000 Wörter nicht überschreitet und die Lehrkraft sicherstellt, dass darin keine Eintragungen durch die Schülerinnen und Schüler vorgenommen wurden. Diese Vorgehensweise ist jedoch wegen des erhöhten Kontrollaufwandes eher unüblich und müsste mit der Oberstufenleitung abgesprochen werden.
Sämtliche Handys, Organizer etc. müssen bei Prüfungsbeginn abgegeben werden, um Täuschungsversuche zu vermeiden. Armbanduhren o. Ä. sind zur Zeitkontrolle erlaubt.

Wie ist die Prüfung aufgebaut?

Die Prüflinge bekommen beide Aufgabenvorschläge ausgehändigt und haben 30 Minuten Zeit, um sich für einen der beiden Vorschläge zu entscheiden. Ihre Auswahl müssen Sie auf den Klausurbögen vermerken.
Die Prüfung umfasst in der Regel drei Bereiche:

1. comprehension
2. analysis
3. evaluation

In jedem Bereich müssen Sie jeweils eine Teilaufgabe bearbeiten. Eine Wahlmöglichkeit ist üblicherweise bei Teilaufgabe 3 vorgesehen. Hier müssen Sie sich zwischen den Aufgabenarten *comment* und *(re-)creation of text* entscheiden. Auch hier kann nur eine der beiden Aufgaben in die Wertung einfließen, unabhängig davon, ob beide bearbeitet worden sind. Entscheiden Sie sich also für **einen** Klausurvorschlag und dann für **eine** der beiden Wahlmöglichkeiten im Wahlbereich dieses Vorschlages!

Was die Ausgangsmaterialien angeht, sind zwei Aufgabenarten möglich:

- Aufgabenart A: Textaufgabe
- Aufgabenart B: Textaufgabe in Kombination mit weiteren Medien (z. B. Statistiken, Diagramme, Schaubilder, bildliche Darstellungen oder Hör- bzw. audiovisuelle Texte)

Die Länge der Ausgangstexte für die Aufgabenart A liegt im GK bei 400–600 und im LK bei 600–800 Wörtern. Bei Aufgabenart B sollten 400 Wörter (GK) bzw. 500 Wörter (LK) nicht überschritten werden. Ein auditiver oder audiovisueller Text sollte eine Länge von drei bis vier Minuten nicht überschreiten. Bei der Verwendung von bildlichen Materialien oder Statistiken sollten nicht mehr als zwei Darstellungen verwendet werden.

Welche Themen werden geprüft?

Die folgenden Unterrichtsinhalte werden in den Aufgaben der schriftlichen Abiturprüfung 2011 vorausgesetzt:

British and American traditions and visions

- British history: From Empire to Commonwealth, monarchy and modern democracy, the UK and Europe
- The American Dream then and now

Globalization – global challenges

- Economic and ecological issues
- International peace-keeping at the turn of the century: the role of the UN and the USA

Post-colonialism and migration

- The post-colonial experience in India
- The role of the New English Literatures: Indian and Pakistani communities in Britain

Shakespeare – a literary 'giant' in the 21st century

- Shakespeare and the Elizabethan World (nur Leistungskurs)
- In-depth study of a play and corresponding film passages/scenes from theatre performances (nur Leistungskurs)
- The interest of young audiences in Shakespeare – passages from a Shakespeare play and from a contemporary film (nur Grundkurs)

Utopia and dystopia – exploring alternative worlds

- Science and ethics: genetic engineering
- Science fiction, fantasy and utopia

Was sind Operatoren und Anforderungsbereiche?

Bei den Aufgaben wird zwischen drei Anforderungsbereichen (AFB) unterschieden:

- In AFB I wird das Textverständis geprüft.
- In AFB II werden Textanalyse und vertiefte Textbearbeitung erwartet.
- In AFB III sollen die Schülerinnen und Schüler im Rückgriff auf ihre erworbenen Fähigkeiten und Fertigkeiten eine Beurteilung der im Text getroffenen Aussagen vornehmen und diese mit weiterem Hintergrundwissen verknüpfen.

Jedem dieser Teilbereiche sind bestimmte Operatoren zugeordnet. Diese verdeutlichen den Prüflingen bereits beim Lesen, welche Kompetenzen sie abrufen müssen bzw. was genau sie in der Aufgabe zu tun haben.

Übersicht über die Operatoren

Anforderungsbereich I

describe	give a detailed account of s.th.	Describe Romeo's situation in the given scene.
		Anforderungsbereich II: Describe the way the author creates an atmosphere of suspense.
outline	give the main features, structure or general principles of a topic omitting minor details	Outline the protagonist's views on designer babies.
state	specify clearly	State briefly the problems of the family described in the text.
present	(re-)structure and write down	Present the situation of the family.
point out	find and explain certain aspects	Point out the author's main ideas on globalization.
summarize, write a summary	give a concise account of the main points	Summarize the information given in the text about the situation in a Chinese sweatshop.

Anforderungsbereich II

analyse, examine	describe and explain in detail certain aspects and/or features of the text	Analyse the speaker's view on the American Dream. Examine the author's use of language.
characterize	describe and examine the way in which the character(s) is/are presented	Characterize/Write a characterization of Jesemin.
examine	cf. analyse	
explain	describe and define in detail	Explain the protagonist's obsession with money.
illustrate	use examples to explain or make clear	Illustrate the author's use of imagery.
interpret	make clear the meaning of s.th.	Interpret the message the author wishes to convey with his poem.
compare	point out similarities and differences	Compare the attitude of the two characters towards the church.

Anforderungsbereich III

comment	state clearly your opinions on the topic in question and support your views with evidence	Comment on the question whether the assimilation of immigrants is preferable to their integration into society.
discuss	investigate or examine by argument; give reasons for and against	Discuss the implications of genetic engineering as presented in the article.
justify	show adequate grounds for decisions or conclusions	You have to give a speech before the press. Justify your decision to send less troops to support the UN.
evaluate	form an opinion after carefully considering and presenting advantages and disadvantages	Evaluate the author's view on the American Dream in today's society.
contrast	emphasize the differences between two or more things	Contrast the protagonist's view on arranged marriages with that of his younger sister.
assess	consider in a balanced way the points for and against s.th.	Assess the importance of freedom of speech in our society.

Wie gehe ich am besten an die Aufgaben heran und worauf sollte ich beim Bearbeiten achten?

Zunächst sollten Sie beide Aufgabenvorschläge gründlich durchlesen und gegebenenfalls unter Zuhilfenahme von Notizen, Mindmaps etc. überlegen, zu welcher Aufgabenstellung Sie mehr schreiben könnten. Hierbei sollten Sie sowohl Ihr Hintergrundwissen als auch Ihr Textverständnis und Ihr Wissen um die durch die Operatoren gesetzten Anforderungen in Betracht ziehen. Ihnen muss genau klar sein, was jeweils von Ihnen verlangt wird.
Haben Sie sich einmal entschieden, bleiben Sie bei dieser Entscheidung!

Nun bleibt es Ihnen überlassen, wie Sie methodisch vorgehen möchten. Sie können zunächst alle drei Aufgaben nacheinander durch mehrfaches Lesen des Textes, verschiedenfarbige Markierungen im Text und Notizen vorbereiten und danach die entsprechenden Texte verfassen. Oder aber Sie bearbeiten alle drei Aufgaben nacheinander.

Ein guter Tipp könnte folgende Vorgehensweise sein:

- Lesen Sie den Text jeweils gezielt hinsichtlich der in der Aufgabe gestellten Anforderungen (Operatoren!) durch und markieren Sie entsprechende Passagen.
- Strukturieren Sie Ihre Notizen so, dass Sie eine sinnvolle Abfolge von *paragraphs* in Ihren Texten erhalten.

Aufgabe 1:

- Nennen Sie in einem Einleitungssatz Autor, Titel, Textart und Entstehungsjahr des Textes.
- Beachten Sie im Hauptteil Ihrer Antwort, dass Sie in diesem Aufgabenbereich weder zitieren noch analysieren oder kommentieren dürfen.

Aufgaben 2 und 3:

- Formulieren Sie aussagekräftige Einleitungssätze/Thesen, in denen Sie sich auf die Aufgabenstellung beziehen.
- Suchen Sie Textpassagen heraus, die Ihre Ausführungen stützen und zitieren Sie diese. Beachten Sie dabei die Regeln für korrektes Zitieren: Setzen Sie wörtliche Zitate immer in Anführungszeichen und geben Sie bei allen Belegen stets die genaue Fundstelle (z. B. l. 17 oder ll. 20–25) an.
- Formulieren Sie unbedingt eine zusammenfassende Conclusio am Ende Ihrer Essays.
- Nutzen Sie Ihr Hintergrundwissen, um Sachverhalte zu erläutern und zu vertiefen. Hierbei kann es sich anbieten, kurz stichpunktartig zu notieren, was Sie zusätzlich zu den im Text genannten Informationen zum Thema wissen. Dadurch können Ihnen weitere Zusammenhänge ein- oder auffallen, die Ihnen bei der Bearbeitung der Fragestellung helfen.

Wie wird die Arbeit bewertet und wie viel zählt sie für die Endnote?

Im Allgemeinen wird die Klausur von einem Erstgutachter (dem/der unterrichtenden Lehrer/in) und danach von einem Zweitgutachter korrigiert und bewertet. Der Zweitgutachter kann von derselben Schule kommen oder extern, d. h. von einer anderen Schule, herangezogen werden. Ob die Zweitkorrektur innerhalb einer Schule oder extern durchgeführt wird, wird zentral festgelegt.
Bei der Korrektur gelten die allgemeinen Richtlinien zur Bewertung von schriftlichen Prüfungsleistungen. Den Korrektoren sind Erwartungshorizonte mit einem Punkteraster vorgegeben, nach dessen Kriterien sie die Klausuren bewerten müssen. Dabei wird zwischen der inhaltlichen und der sprachlichen Leistung unterschieden.
Weichen die beiden Korrektoren in ihrer Punktevergabe um bis zu drei Notenpunkte voneinander ab, so wird das arithmetische Mittel aus beiden Noten gebildet. Beträgt die Abweichung vier Notenpunkte oder mehr, so wird ein Drittkorrektor eingesetzt, dessen Beurteilung dann entscheidet.

Die vier Prüfungsergebnisse in den Abiturprüfungsfächern fließen in fünffacher Wertung in die Endnote ein. Wird zusätzlich eine besondere Lernleistung erbracht, werden die Prüfungsergebnisse in den Prüfungsfächern vierfach gewertet und das Ergebnis der besonderen Lernleistung in vierfacher Wertung hinzugezählt. Wird im ersten bis dritten Abiturfach sowohl schriftlich als auch mündlich geprüft, wird das Endergebnis im Verhältnis von 2 (schriftlich) zu 1 (mündlich) aus den Ergebnissen der beiden Prüfungsteile gebildet. Ein Leistungsausgleich zwischen den zwei Bereichen ist nicht möglich.

Kann man sich noch mündlich prüfen lassen?

Sie können sich noch mündlich prüfen lassen, wenn das Ergebnis der schriftlichen Arbeit sich um vier oder mehr Punkte von dem Durchschnitt der Punkte unterscheidet, die Sie in den für die Gesamtqualifikation verbindlichen Kursen des jeweiligen Prüfungsfaches in den vier Halbjahren der Qualifikationsphase erreicht haben, oder wenn das Bestehen der Abiturprüfung gefährdet ist, weil die vorgeschriebenen Mindestbedingungen nicht erfüllt sind. Eine mündliche Prüfung wird nicht durchgeführt, wenn aufgrund der vorliegenden Ergebnisse im Abiturbereich auch bei Erreichen der Höchstpunktzahl in der mündlichen Prüfung im ersten bis dritten Abiturfach ein Bestehen des Abiturs nicht mehr möglich ist.

PRÜFUNGSAUFGABEN 2008

Aufgabentyp	Textaufgabe: comprehension, analysis, evaluation
Thema/ Schwerpunkt	Post-colonialism and migration: The post-colonial experience in India The role of the New English literatures: Indian and Pakistani communities in Britain
Material	Manil Suri: The Death of Vishnu
Textsorte	Literarischer Text: Romanauszug

Aufgabe I

Aufgabenstellung:

1 Describe the preparations for the marriage and the young couple's behaviour and feelings. **(Comprehension) (16 Punkte)**

2 Analyse the way in which Manil Suri portrays the arranged marriage. In doing so, consider setting, mode of presentation, point of view and characterization. **(Analysis) (24 Punkte)**

3 Choose <u>one</u> of the following tasks:

3.1 Against the background of the current debate on a "clash of cultures", compare the type of marriage described in this text with the different ways of finding a partner in the film *Bend it Like Beckham,* and comment on the future of marriage traditions in a multicultural society. **(Evaluation: comment) (20 Punkte)**

3.2 Fill the gap in line 31 with Vinod's thoughts at this moment. Make sure that your addition helps the reader to understand Vinod's views of the events and fits in with Vinod's character and the narrative style of the text. **(Evaluation: re-creation of text) (20 Punkte)**

Text

Extract from Manil Suri's novel *The Death of Vishnu* (2001)

Vinod Taneja, a widower, lives in an apartment block in Mumbai, India. The following extract describes how he and his wife met and prepared for their wedding night.

On the day Vinod passed his Bachelor of Commerce exam, his father announced they had found a suitable match for him. Would he have any objection to marrying Sheetal, the niece of his uncle's wife, who had been at Paplu's birthday party last week?

Vinod remembered seeing her there. He hadn't paid her any attention, nor had he tried to talk to her, although he was sure he had said hello once at a previous family function. She was not the most beautiful woman he had laid eyes on, but on the other hand, he couldn't remember any obvious physical defects either. Thinking about it overnight, he could come up with no particular reason to either reject or endorse the match. The wedding was negotiated that very week.

A few days later, he found himself at the house of his future in-laws. Sheetal's mother brought out the sets of jewelry that were to be given with the bride and laid them out for his family's inspection. His mother put on her reading glasses, and lifting the pieces from their red velvet boxes, started examining them one by one. Vinod watched the proceedings for a while, and then, with nothing to do, picked up a necklace himself, and held it up against his palm.

He was trying to follow a point of light as it skittered from stone to stone when his eyes met Sheetal's. He was startled by the disdain in them, a disdain so keen he had to look away. He put the necklace down immediately, then tried to catch Sheetal's eye again. But she did not look up, keeping her face properly lowered through the rest of the meeting.

He saw her next a few weeks after that, at their engagement. He wanted to talk to Sheetal then, but their eyes did not meet once during the entire ceremony. Even when he offered her the laddoo, Sheetal did not raise her head, but waited for him to bring it to her mouth, so she could take a delicate bite.

The period between the engagement and wedding passed by in a haze. Vinod spent the days at his new job in the bank, and his evenings as before, gathering with friends at the café near Churchgate. There were many jokes about his impending union, but somehow he managed not to think about how his life was going to change. The wedding always seemed to be at least a few days away, and Vinod occupied his hours without letting himself worry about it.

It was only when he saw his garments being tied to Sheetal's that the enormity and irreversibility of the situation hit him. He was getting married, and he did not know why, or to whom. He looked up at the guests and relatives all around and heard them whispering and saw them smiling at him. [...]

And then he was entering their wedding-night room and closing the door, the sounds of giggling were left outside, and the bride was sitting on the petal-strewn bed. He had seen this scene so many times before - Raj Kapoor and Nargis, Guru Dutt and Waheeda Rehman, Dilip Kumar and Madhubala, the heroine always in embroidered silk, the groom in impeccable white, and when the hero pulled back the heroine's ghunghat, she kept her eyes closed. He reached out to lift the cloth, and his hand wavered. What if Sheetal's eyes were staring at his, defiant, with the look of that first day? But his wife must have seen the same films he had, because when he looked under the cloth, her eyes were closed, the dots painted in ceremonial white forming a serene arch over her eyebrows. For a second, he wondered if he should break into song as they did in the movies. Instead, he lifted her head slowly, and asked her to open her eyes.

In that first clear look into the eyes of the person with whom he was supposed to spend the rest of his life, he was relieved to find not defiance but curiosity, not disdain but unfamiliarity, not love but not dislike, either. [...]

They sat there next to each other, the layers of clothing and ornaments they were wearing too intimidating to allow conversation, let alone intimacy. More daunting was the fact that they had met only twice since the engagement, that too under the supervision of a caucus of chaperons. The silence pressed around them, as oppressive as the heat and the humidity in the air.

751 words

Manil Suri: The Death of Vishnu, London: Bloomsbury, 2001, pp. 199 - 202

Annotations

1 Bachelor of Commerce: the basic college/university degree in the field of economics
5 function: *here:* social event
21 laddoo: ball-shaped Indian sweet
25 Churchgate: business area in Mumbai (formerly known as Bombay, the biggest city in India) with a lot of offices and banks
28 garments being tied: in a Hindu wedding ceremony first the scarves of the bride and the bridegroom are tied together as a symbol of their union and then the couple walks seven times around a fire and takes the seven wedding promises
34 Raj Kapoor etc.: popular Indian film actors and actresses
36 ghunghat: *(Hindi)* cloth worn by a bride to hide her face

Aufgabentyp	Textaufgabe: comprehension, analysis, evaluation
Thema/ Schwerpunkt	Globalization – global challenges: Economic and ecological issues – towards sustainable development International peace-keeping at the turn of the century: the role of the UN and the USA Post-colonialism and migration: The post-colonial experience in India
Material	Tony Blair's Lord Mayor's Banquet Speech
Textsorte	Sach- und Gebrauchstext: Politische Rede

Aufgabe II

Aufgabenstellung:

1 Outline Tony Blair's view of globalisation, the global challenges of our time and necessary political answers. **(Comprehension) (16 Punkte)**

2 Explain how the Prime Minister uses argumentative structure, language and rhetorical devices to convince the audience of his view on globalisation.
(Analysis) (24 Punkte)

3 Choose one of the following tasks:

3.1 In lines 47 – 49 Tony Blair states: "In a modern world there is no security or prosperity at home unless we deal with the global challenges of conflict, terrorism, climate change and poverty. Self interest and mutual interest are inextricably linked. National interests can best be advanced through collective action." Comment on this statement and its implications for the richest countries and for yourself.
(Evaluation: comment) (20 Punkte)

3.2 After Tony Blair's speech, a political representative of India who is a guest of honour at the dinner is invited by the host, the Lord Mayor of London, to give a speech in response to the Prime Minister's speech. Write the speech.
(Evaluation: re-creation of text) (20 Punkte)

Text

Tony Blair's Lord Mayor's Banquet Speech

During a traditional dinner at the Guildhall in London on November 14, 2005, British Prime Minister Tony Blair made a major world affairs speech.

Thirty years ago a political leader who said that the way to advance the national interest was through the spread, worldwide, of the values of democracy, justice and liberty, would have been called an idealist.

Today such a person is a realist. We describe the modern world as interdependent. We acknowledge the force of globalisation. But we fail to follow through the logic of these realities in global politics.

Nations are deeply connected at every level. Of course, economically, but also now through communication, travel and technology.

Yesterday, by chance, I watched part of the MTV Music Awards. Well, it was certainly the most relaxed part of the week I just had. I recommend it to any person who wants to understand modern politics. Why? There was no politics discussed. But the fusion of sounds, rhythms and musical influences from vastly different cultures was an allegory for today's world and the context in which politics exists. This is a world integrating at a fast rate, with enormous economic, cultural and political consequences.

And it all happens as a result of what people themselves are doing. Occasionally we debate globalisation as if it were something imposed by governments or business on unwilling people. Wrong. It is the individual decisions of millions of people that is creating and driving globalisation. Globalisation isn't something done to us. It is something we are, consciously or unconsciously, doing to and for ourselves.

[...]

... out of this great pumping up of global integration comes the need for stronger and more effective global, multilateral action. There is a real danger that the institutions of global politics lag seriously behind the challenges they are called upon to resolve.

These challenges are pressing. The most obvious is global terrorism. Barely a week goes by without another country being added to the grieving list of victims. Jordan, Egypt, Indonesia, India and of course here in London. Recently, in Australia, it appears an attack was foiled. We have disrupted two groups planning attacks here in the UK since 7 July alone. What is obvious now to all is that this is a global movement and requires global action in response, of which the successful completion of a democratic process in Afghanistan and Iraq is a major component. So is the push for peace between Israel and Palestine. In all of these conflicts, the only successful solution is based on democratic consent; and success would have a tremendous persuasive effect far beyond the frontiers of the countries concerned.

Similarly, with the challenge of climate change, the world has to act together. After Gleneagles we began the G8 + 5 talks with the first meeting in London on November 1. The commitment period under the Kyoto protocol ends in 2012. We urgently need a framework, with the necessary targets, sensitively and intelligently applied over the right timeframe, that takes us beyond 2012.

It can only happen if the US, China and India join with Europe, Japan and others to create such a framework. Failure will mean not only increasing the damage to the environment but in a world of greater competition for carbon fuel, real pressure on energy supply and energy prices. Yet such an agreement cannot materialize without the major nations of the world agreeing an approach that is fair and balanced, sharing the most advanced science and technology to tackle carbon emissions. In other words, a just settlement as well as an effective one.

And we surely know already that if we leave millions of the world's poorest out of the onward march of global prosperity, we do not merely indicate moral indifference, but commit a foolish betrayal of our own long-term interest. [...]

In a modern world there is no security or prosperity at home unless we deal with the global challenges of conflict, terrorism, climate change and poverty. Self interest and mutual interest are inextricably linked. National interests can best be advanced through collective action.

Calculate not just the human misery of the poor themselves. Calculate our loss: the aid, the lost opportunity to trade, the short-term consequences of the multiple conflicts; the long-term consequences on the attitude to the wealthy world of injustice and abject deprivation amongst the poor. We will reap what we sow; live with what we do not act to change.

Here, in the City of London, which makes its living above all by being the meeting point of many nations, and which through trade creates much of the wealth on which this British nation depends, is a good place for this call to action. So let us act.

764 words

Tony Blair's Lord Mayor's Banquet Speech, November 14, 2005
Internet: http://www.number-10.gov.uk/output/Page8524.asp [zuletzt aufgerufen am 01.07.2010]

Annotations

12 allegory: *here:* typical example

33 Gleneagles: a hotel in Scotland; *here:* the G8-summit in July, 2005, where the heads of government of Canada, France, Germany, Italy, Japan, Russia, the United Kingdom and the United States met to discuss international problems

34 G8 + 5 talks: the meeting of the eight politicians with the political leaders of Brazil, China, India, Mexico and South Africa

34/35 commitment period: a period of time for which plans and promises have been made

35 the Kyoto protocol: an international agreement from February 16, 2005 to reduce greenhouse gas emission worldwide

LÖSUNGSVORSCHLAG 2008

Aufgabe I

1 Comprehension: Describe the preparations ...

HINWEIS In dieser Aufgabe werden Sie gebeten, textbezogen drei Bereiche des Themas *arranged marriages* zu beschreiben: *preparations for the marriage, the young couple's behaviour, their feelings.*

NÜTZLICHE WENDUNGEN **Operator *describe***
- to be presented as ...
- to appear to be ...
- to be seemingly ...
- to depict s. th.
- to portray s. o./s. th.
- to represent s. th.

Lösungsschritte zu Aufgabe 1

1	Prüfen Sie die verwendeten Operatoren. Diese geben Ihnen genaue Informationen darüber, was Sie in der Aufgabe zu leisten haben (hier: *describe*).
2	Aktivieren Sie bereits vor dem ersten Lesen des Textes Ihr Hintergrundwissen und scannen Sie ihn dann gezielt nach Informationen zu den drei zu untersuchenden Aspekten. Markieren Sie diese entweder farbig im Text oder notieren Sie sie tabellarisch.
3	Unterstreichen Sie die wichtigen Fakten (keine Details, Beispiele, wörtliche Rede, Aufzählungen).
4	Benennen Sie Autor, Titel, Textart und Entstehungsjahr in Ihrem Einleitungssatz.
5	Lösen Sie sich vom Text und formulieren Sie eine kurze Zusammenfassung in eigenen Worten. Denken Sie an die Verwendung des *Simple Present* und von Konnektoren, damit die logischen Zusammenhänge deutlich werden.
6	Vermeiden Sie in diesem Aufgabenbereich Kommentare, persönliche Wertungen oder Analysen.
7	Beachten Sie, dass Sie weder wörtliche Rede noch Zitate verwenden dürfen.
8	Strukturieren Sie Ihren Text in *paragraphs,* welche jeweils nur einen Aspekt beinhalten sollten.

NÜTZLICHE WENDUNGEN **Konnektoren/connectors**
- in the beginning
- firstly/secondly
- then/after that/later in the text
- finally/in conclusion
- although
- besides
- moreover/furthermore
- either ... or/neither ... nor
- despite/in spite of this

Stichpunktlösung zu Aufgabe 1

Preparations for the marriage:

- the parents arrange everything from choosing the partners to negotiating the marriage portion
- the couple is present as well but does not have any say in the procedure
- the couple does not know each other beforehand, having seen each other only once
- the groom is asked if he has any objections to the marriage but as he cannot find strong arguments for or against the marriage, he accepts his parents' choice
- the preparations follow a fixed set of meetings with determined roles for parents and couple, i. e. preliminary meeting of the parents, meeting with parents and couple, engagement, marriage

The young couple's behaviour:

- the relationship of Vinod and Sheetal develops in the course of this extract: at the beginning they are rather distanced from each other but slowly they begin to overcome this distance
- at first Vinod is not really interested in his future bride
- when they meet officially he is polite but still distanced, they do not speak to each other
- she behaves properly, acts very demure
- during the engagement ceremony and later in the wedding-night room Vinod tries to connect with her by eye-contact; again Sheetal is reserved and passive

The couple's feelings:

Vinod	Sheetal
■ he is at first indifferent to his bride ■ shortly before the wedding he suppresses his developing doubts about his chosen future ■ in the wedding-night room he is insecure, because he cannot predict his wife's reaction to him ■ looking into her eyes he feels relieved as he reads her emotions	■ watching him playing with one of the necklaces from her dowry she shows disdain ■ in the course of the other meetings she is reserved ■ in the bedroom her eyes show curiosity about her husband

2 Analysis: Analyse the way in which Manil Suri portrays ...

HINWEIS In der Analyse sind Sie gebeten, die **Darstellungsweise** des Themas *arranged marriage* zu analysieren. Zu diesem Zweck müssen Sie die unterschiedlichen in der Aufgabenstellung benannten Teilaspekte analysieren und ihre Funktion erläutern.

Lösungsschritte zu Aufgabe 2

1	Prüfen Sie die verwendeten Operatoren. Diese geben Ihnen genaue Informationen darüber, was Sie in der Aufgabe zu leisten haben (hier: *analyse*).
2	Scannen Sie den Text und Ihre Aufzeichnungen nach relevanten Teilinformationen: *setting (place/time), mode of presentation (scenic vs. panoramic presentation), point of view (first-person narrator, third-person narrator, omniscient perspective [unlimited narrative perspective or limited point of view], characterization (outward appearance, behaviour, social background, thoughts, statements ...).* Benennen Sie, was Ihnen darüber hinaus noch auffällt.
3	Unterstreichen oder notieren Sie aussagekräftige Beispiele.
4	Formulieren Sie einen Einleitungssatz mit einer These zur Art der Präsentation des Themenbereiches *arranged marriage.*
5	Erläutern Sie jeweils auch die **Funktion** und **Wirkung** der von Ihnen analysierten Aspekte. Dies bedeutet, dass Sie bei der Benennung der Erzählperspektive ***(third-person narrator)*** auch erläutern müssen, welche Konsequenzen diese limitierte Perspektive auf die Darstellung der Situation und folglich auch auf das Verständnis des Lesers hat.

6	Strukturieren Sie Ihren Text in *paragraphs,* welche jeweils nur einen Aspekt beinhalten sollten.
7	Vergessen Sie nicht, am Ende eine zusammenfassende Conclusio zu formulieren.

NÜTZLICHE WENDUNGEN **Textanalyse/analysis**
- the scene is set in ...
- scenic presentation/panoramic presentation
- the narrator gives a scenic/panoramic presentation of ...
- first-person narrator with a limited point of view/a selective omniscience (third-person omniscient narrator/third-person limited narrator)
- narrated by a third-person omniscient narrator
- direct characterization/indirect characterization
- characterized directly/indirectly
- direct speech/reported speech/reported thought

Stichpunktlösung zu Aufgabe 2

Setting:
- the (cultural) area is the India of today, more precisely Mumbai and its economic centre Churchgate
- the house of Sheetal's family, where the couple is only witnessing the events
- the wedding chamber from which escape is impossible but which provides the first opportunity to get acquainted with each other

Mode of presentation:
- **scenic presentation** of key events and moments of the preparation for the wedding and the wedding night, i.e. proposal of Vinod's father, the first meeting, the engagement, the wedding ceremony, the wedding night
- **panoramic presentation** of what happens over a period of time between the engagement and the wedding; this underlines Vinod's attempt to repress his fear of what will come next and the fast approach of the wedding

Point of view:
- third-person narrator with a selective omniscience or a limited point of view
- the reader gets direct insight into Vinod's emotions and thoughts
- Sheetal is presented subjectively, through Vinod's eyes
- the focus is on Vinod, leading the reader to identify with his view of the events described

Characterization:

- direct characterization (through Vinod and the narrator)
- indirect characterization (mostly of Vinod, but also of Sheetal and Vinod's parents)

Vinod	Sheetal	Vinod's parents
educated, at the beginning of his career, traditional values, "normal" young man (meeting friends in the evening), doubting his parents' decisions only after agreeing first	appears unobtrusive, very much adapted to social conventions, views the wedding preparations at the beginning with (hidden) disdain, in the wedding chamber she signals both willingness to adapt to the new situation and curiosity	very traditional, stick to their respective roles

Further features:

- the lack of direct speech creates a certain distance to the events and accelerates the course of events
- Vinod's thoughts, reactions and fears are presented in reported thought, again creating a slight distance between protagonist and reader
- the question of Vinod's father as to whether he would marry Sheetal is a rhetorical question; the father was sure of his son's acceptance

3.1 Comment: Against the background ..., compare ... and comment on ...

HINWEIS Falls Sie diese Aufgabe gewählt haben, sind Sie angehalten, die Zukunft von traditionellen Eheschließungen zu kommentieren. Dabei sollen Sie der Diskussion über den *clash of cultures* in multikulturellen Gesellschaften besondere Beachtung schenken. Sie sollen außerdem Ihr Hintergrundwissen über Partnerwahl in *Bend it like Beckham* mit einbeziehen und mit dem vorliegenden Romanausschnitt vergleichen.

Lösungsschritte zu Aufgabe 3.1

1	Prüfen Sie die verwendeten Operatoren und Hinweise. Diese geben Ihnen genaue Informationen darüber, was Sie in der Aufgabe zu leisten haben (hier: *comment on* und *compare*).
2	Scannen Sie den Text und Ihre Aufzeichnungen kurz nach relevanten Teilinformationen und überlegen Sie, was Sie zusätzlich aus den durchgeführten Unterrichtsreihen wissen: *arranged marriage, looking for a partner/courtship today, development in a multicultural society.*
3	Unterstreichen oder notieren Sie aussagekräftige Beispiele.
4	Machen Sie sich Ihre persönliche Einstellung zu diesem Thema klar und formulieren Sie diese prägnant und anschaulich.
5	Formulieren Sie einen Einleitungssatz, in dem Sie eine erste These zur Entwicklung der *marriage traditions* anführen.
6	Bauen Sie Ihren Essay sachlogisch auf und verbinden Sie Ihre Gedankengänge mit passenden Konnektoren.
7	Benennen Sie jeweils passende Belege und Beispiele zur Untermauerung Ihrer Ausführungen.
8	Strukturieren Sie Ihren Text in *paragraphs,* welche jeweils nur einen Aspekt beinhalten sollten.
9	Vergessen Sie nicht, am Ende eine zusammenfassende Conclusio zu formulieren.

Stichpunktlösung zu Aufgabe 3.1

Presenting arranged marriages in their context of the corresponding cultural areas (extract from *The Death of Vishnu*):

- rules and traditions of arranged marriages are apparently that parents arrange everything, there is a clearly prescribed way of acting for all participants, partner is usually from the same community or caste, bride and groom only really get to know each other after the wedding

Comparing different forms of finding a partner in London in the 1990s – still with respect to Indian culture (film *Bend it like Beckham*):

- Jess and Joe: they hide their love, still there is a normal courtship across cultures, mutual attraction to each other despite cultural differences; Jess only superficially fulfills the traditional role of an Indian woman
- Pinky and Teetu: they want to fulfill their parents' expectations of a traditional wedding ceremony; Pinky seems to personify the modern version of a traditional

woman, still when the wedding is endangered, both overstep the rules to see each other; in this case the traditional ceremony only followed the love of the two

HINWEIS Nun sollten Sie einen der vorher genannten Aspekte auswählen und mögliche Entwicklungen herausarbeiten.

Speculating about possible changes to marriage traditions in a multicultural society:

- the fusion of traditional ceremony (arranged marriage) and marriage for love depicted in *Bend it like Beckham* might appear more often
- people can choose partners from more than just their own cultural background: the use of dating sites on the Internet, meeting people from all over the world at universities, the growing number of people from different cultures who come to live together
- the fascination with Bollywood that has opened western minds to Indian culture – even though the presentation is often very exaggerated

Stating personal opinion concerning the clash of cultures:

- it is always a matter of carefully balancing the attempt to keep your own cultural identity and the will to integrate into the culture of the country you are living in
- there is no model solution stating in which respects one should assimilate and which aspects one has to keep in order to create a cohesive view of the world
- one has to find a compromise between one's own cultural heritage and that of the new country

3.2 Re-creation of text: Fill the gap in line 31 with Vinod's thoughts ...

HINWEIS Diese Aufgabe verlangt von Ihnen eine sprachliche und inhaltliche Arbeit auf mehreren Ebenen: Sie müssen sich in Stil und Formulierungen möglichst nahe am Originaltext halten. Gleichzeitig wird von Ihnen verlangt, die Perspektive Vinods glaubhaft und nahe an den im Text angelegten Eigenschaften, Einstellungen und Entwicklungsmöglichkeiten des Charakters zu gestalten.

Lösungsschritte zu Aufgabe 3.2

1	Prüfen Sie die verwendeten Operatoren und Hinweise. Diese geben Ihnen genaue Informationen darüber, was Sie in der Aufgabe zu leisten haben (hier: *fill in the gap ... understand Vinod's view of the events ... fits in with ... character ... style of the text*).
2	Scannen Sie den Text und Ihre Aufzeichnungen kurz nach relevanten Teilinformationen: *character, style (reported stream of thought: questions, fears etc. of Vinod*).
3	Unterstreichen oder notieren Sie aussagekräftige Beispiele.
4	Lösen Sie sich von Ihrem wissenschaftlichen Schreibstil und lassen Sie sich auf den Erzählstil von Manil Suri ein.

Stichpunktlösung zu Aufgabe 3.2

Vinod's thoughts:

- he knows the situation cannot be reversed, the wedding will take place no matter what
- he is also aware of his parents' expectations and of the "protocol"
- he knows about the importance of the situation for all those present

Vinod's view of the events, connected to concrete events in the past or in the future:

- he might doubt whether the marriage will be successful
- he might feel slightly rebellious, wishing he had not consented to his parents' wishes
- he might be afraid of being alone with his wife later
- he reflects on the events that led to the wedding and asks himself where or how he could have reacted differently

Presenting Vinod according to his characterization (cf. your own results in the analysis):

- Vinod is an academic; at the same time he is bound to the old traditions of his parents and, being very reserved or conservative, he does not blindly follow his parents' instructions but eventually reflects on his situation

> TIPP Versuchen Sie, beim Verfassen Ihrer Lösung den Schreibstil des Autors nachzuahmen und Vinods Fragen, Ängste und Träume in einem *reported stream of thought* darzustellen.

Ausführlicher Lösungsvorschlag zu Aufgabe 3.2

And then he felt weak and faint. Everything had gone so quickly. Without even thinking much he had simply consented to his father's wishes. But wasn't that what a son should do? For a moment he felt torn between knowing that pleasing his parents and living according to the ancient rules and traditions was honouring his family and earning them the respect of their community. And he felt happy about doing this. But at the same time he couldn't help wondering what his feelings would be like if he had gone out with a girl from university and fallen in love with her. This DID happen in movies. He might even have had the courage to propose to her - but then ...? It wasn't that he regretted sitting next to Sheetal and getting married. She was quite beautiful. She acted appropriately. She pleased his parents. But what if the second of pure disdain that he had seen in her eyes during that first meeting unleashed as soon as they were alone? What if she could not like him?

(180 words)

Schnell-Check zu Aufgabe I

Auf-gabe	Thema/Aufgabentyp			Trainingstipps
1	*Describe ...* Im Text dargestellte Sachverhalte beschreiben			■ Üben Sie, einen Text nach relevanten Informationen zu scannen. ■ Wiederholen Sie die Kriterien zum Verfassen einer *summary*. ■ Schlagen Sie themenrelevantes Vokabular nach, um sich sprachlich vorzubereiten. ■ Wiederholen Sie Konnektoren, um Ihren Text logisch zu strukturieren.
2	*Analyse ...* Die Erzählweise des Autors analysieren			■ Wiederholen Sie das entsprechende Fachvokabular für folgende Bereiche: *setting, mode of presentation, point of view, characterization.* ■ Üben Sie Formulierungen, in denen Sie z. B. den gewählten *point of view* benennen und dessen Funktion bzw. Wirkung auf den Leser erläutern. ■ Üben Sie das Formulieren von *paragraphs*.
3.1	*Comment on ...* Ein im Text dargestell-tes Thema kommentieren			■ Sehen Sie Ihre Unterlagen durch und erstellen Sie Begriffsnetze oder Mindmaps, um Ihr Wissen und Ihren Lernstoff zu vernetzen. ■ Üben Sie, die verschiedenen Einzelbe-reiche in einer sinnvollen Reihenfolge zu verknüpfen, sodass die einzelnen Paragrafen sachlogisch aufeinander aufbauen. ■ Wiederholen Sie die Kriterien zum Verfassen eines Essays.
3.2	*Fill in the gap ...* Eine Situation fortführen und dabei die Erzählweise des Autors nachahmen			■ Üben Sie, Texte im Stil des Autors weiterzuschreiben. Machen Sie sich dazu jeweils Notizen über stilistische und sprachliche Besonderheiten (z.B. *uses reported thought, register: colloquial*).

Aufgabe II

1 Comprehension: Outline Tony Blair's view of globalization ...

HINWEIS In der Aufgabenstellung werden Sie gebeten, textbezogen die Aussagen Tony Blairs zu drei Aspekten der Rede auszuführen: *globalization, global challenges of our time* und *neccessary political answers.*

NÜTZLICHE WENDUNGEN **Operator *outline***
- to be presented as ...
- to appear to be ...
- to be seemingly ...
- to depict s.th.
- to portray s.o./s.th.
- to represent s.th.

Lösungsschritte zu Aufgabe 1

1	Prüfen Sie die verwendeten Operatoren. Diese geben Ihnen genaue Informationen darüber, was Sie in der Aufgabe zu leisten haben (hier: *outline*).
2	Aktivieren Sie bereits vor dem ersten Lesen des Textes Ihr Hintergrundwissen und scannen Sie ihn dann gezielt nach Informationen zu den drei zu untersuchenden Aspekten. Markieren Sie diese entweder farbig im Text oder notieren Sie sie tabellarisch.
3	Unterstreichen Sie die wichtigen Fakten (keine Details, Beispiele, wörtliche Rede, Aufzählungen).
4	Benennen Sie Autor, Titel, Textart und Entstehungsjahr in Ihrem Einleitungssatz.
5	Lösen Sie sich vom Text und formulieren Sie eine kurze Zusammenfassung in eigenen Worten. Denken Sie an die Verwendung des *Simple Present* und von Konnektoren, damit die logischen Zusammenhänge deutlich werden.
6	Vermeiden Sie in diesem Aufgabenbereich Kommentare, persönliche Wertungen oder Analysen.
7	Beachten Sie, dass Sie weder wörtliche Rede noch Zitate verwenden dürfen.
8	Strukturieren Sie Ihren Text in *paragraphs,* welche jeweils nur einen Aspekt beinhalten sollten.

NÜTZLICHE WENDUNGEN **Konnektoren/connectors**
- in the beginning
- firstly/secondly
- then/after that/later in the text
- finally/in conclusion
- although
- besides
- moreover/furthermore
- either ... or/neither ... nor
- despite/in spite of this

Stichpunktlösung zu Aufgabe 1

Globalization:
- there is a global interdependence and networks are established among nations
- the process of globalization advances quickly and has dramatic consequences
- people are taking part actively in this process and are thereby shaping their lives

Global challenges of our time:
- there are a lot of global challenges, i.e. global conflicts and terrorism, climate change, poverty, competition for carbon fuel, which require rapid solutions

Necessary political answers:
- according to Blair these global problems call for a framework that needs to be effective, feasible for a long period of time and therefore built upon a multilateral agreement
- this framework is important because it serves personal interests like "prosperity" and "security"
- not having this kind of framework might effect a pressure on energy supplies and prices and further be a sign of moral indifference

2 Analysis: Explain how the Prime Minister uses ...

HINWEIS Sie sollen in dieser Aufgabe erläutern (Operator *explain*), mit welchen sprachlichen und rhetorischen Mitteln Tony Blair das Publikum von seinen Ansichten zum Thema *globalization* zu überzeugen versucht. Die zu bearbeitenden Analysebereiche sind: *argumentative structure, language* und *rhetorical devices.*

NÜTZLICHE WENDUNGEN **Operator *explain***
- to make use of/to employ a rhetorical device
- to emphasize/stress an argument
- to highlight s.th.
- the use of repetitions/enumerations in line ...
- to make an attitude clear to the reader

Lösungsschritte zu Aufgabe 2

1	Prüfen Sie die verwendeten Operatoren. Diese geben Ihnen genaue Informationen darüber, was Sie in der Aufgabe zu leisten haben (hier: *explain*).
2	Analysieren Sie den Text in mehreren Schritten in Bezug auf die geforderten Teilbereiche *(argumentative structure, language und rhetorical devices).*
3	Rufen Sie sich für die Analyse der argumentativen Struktur Schlüsselbegriffe und typische Strukturelemente für *political speeches* ins Gedächtnis, z. B. *antithesis, sense units.*
4	Die Sprachanalyse *(language)* muss u. a. die Satzstruktur, die verwendete(n) Sprachebene(n), den Gebrauch von Zitaten und den Grad der Anschaulichkeit und Verständlichkeit der Sprache untersuchen.
5	Überlegen Sie, welche rhetorischen Figuren vermehrt in Reden vorkommen und welche Funktionen diese haben können (→ Beispiele siehe **Nützliche Wendungen**).
6	Unterstreichen oder notieren Sie aussagekräftige Beispiele.
7	Formulieren Sie einen Einleitungssatz, in dem Sie sich auf die Aufgabenstellung beziehen.
8	Erläutern Sie immer auch die Funktion und Wirkung der von Ihnen analysierten Aspekte.
9	Strukturieren Sie Ihren Text in *paragraphs,* welche jeweils nur einen Aspekt beinhalten sollten.
10	Vergessen Sie nicht, am Ende eine zusammenfassende Conclusio zu formulieren.

NÜTZLICHE WENDUNGEN **Rhetorische Figuren und Stilmittel/rhetorical and stylistic devices**

- main body
- argument
- thesis (*pl.* theses)
- appeal
- description
- sense unit
- example
- antihesis/contrast
- metaphor
- repetition
- alliteration
- anaphora
- parallelism
- doubles
- the rule of three/tricolon
- amplification
- euphemism
- allusion
- meter
- rhyme
- sentence structure
- connotation
- biblical quote
- colloquial/formal English

Stichpunktlösung zu Aufgabe 2

Argumentative structure:

examples from the speech	effect
■ the text is divided into plausible sense units: introduction to the topic (historical development), description of globalization and example, appeal/thesis, global challenges (examples and answers, self-interest and national interest in the topic, call to action)	■ clear structuring of the argumentation
■ the speaker makes use of antitheses/ contrasts: "Thirty years ago ... Today ..."; "... something imposed by... Wrong."; "Globalisation isn't something done to us. It is something we are ... doing to and for ourselves."	■ pointing out developments or alternatives

Language:

examples from the speech	effect
■ the speech contains immediately understandable and well-known expressions like "march of global prosperity" ■ there is also a biblical quote: "We will reap what we sow." ■ the sentence structure is not very complex, there are even one-word sentences	■ easily understandable and vivid language
■ the speaker employs negatively connoted expressions: "moral indifference"; "a foolish betrayal" ■ negative consequences and unacceptable alternatives are discribed: "Failure will mean…"; "if we leave millions of the world's poorest out of …"	■ the speaker's intention, i.e. to address the global challenges at hand, is presented as important and urgent

Rhetorical devices:

examples from the speech	effect
■ there are informal expressions ("well") ■ the speaker makes humorous remarks: "it was certainly the most relaxed part of the week …" ■ the speaker uses an *inclusive we* ("we", "us", "our") ■ he also directly appeals to his audience: "Calculate …"; "So let us act …"	■ the speaker establishes a somewhat personal relationship, which makes the audience more prone to listen and agree to his arguments
■ **enumeration** of countries where there are victims of terrorism	■ the speaker uses this enumeration to stress the importance of his statement that the most obvious challenge is fighting terrorism
■ **anaphora:** "Calculate … Calculate …"	■ this makes a lasting impression on the audience; stressed in this way a statement is much easier to remember
■ a change of the regular sentence structure: *What is obvious now to all is that …*	■ this emphasizes that finally everybody has understood that these were no isolated incidents and that it is "a global movement which requires global action"

examples from the speech	effect
■ **adverbs** ("seriously"; "urgently") and **adjectives** ("pressing")	■ these also underline the importance of the speaker's deliberations, because the situation requires action

3.1 Comment: In lines ... Comment on this statement ...

HINWEIS Sie sollen das vorgestellte Zitat erläutern und aus zwei Perspektiven kommentieren. Zum einen sollen Sie die in Blairs Rede dargestellten Implikationen für die reichen (westlichen) Industrieländer aufzählen und kommentieren und zum anderen diejenigen, die sich für Sie persönlich ergeben.

Lösungsschritte zu Aufgabe 3.1

1	Prüfen Sie die verwendeten Operatoren. Diese geben Ihnen genaue Informationen darüber, was Sie in der Aufgabe zu leisten haben (hier: *comment on*).
2	Sammeln und erläutern Sie (tabellarisch oder in einer Mindmap) im Textauszug genannte oder angedeutete Konsequenzen von Blairs Forderung.
3	Ergänzen Sie zusätzlich Ihre eigenen Überlegungen. Achten Sie darauf, dass Sie systematisieren und dabei klar zwischen den zwei Anforderungsebenen (persönliche Implikationen, Implikationen für reiche Industrieländer) differenzieren.
4	Bringen Sie Ihre Ergebnisse in eine sinnvolle Reihenfolge. Gut ist hierbei, wenn Sie das jeweils beste Argument am Schluss benennen.
5	Formulieren Sie eine aussagekräftige These in der Einleitung Ihres Essays.
6	Vergessen Sie nicht, Ihre Thesen zu erläutern und mit Beispielen zu veranschaulichen.
7	Denken Sie daran, am Ende eine zusammenfassende Conclusio zu formulieren.

Stichpunktlösung zu Aufgabe 3.1

- Blair's thesis that **national interests** require dealing with global challenges like conflict, terrorism, climate change and poverty is right insofar as all the apects he has mentioned influence everyone in the same way: national security is endangered by a global network of terrorism, therefore Britain has been assisting the US in the Iraq War; national prosperity is endangered by a limitation of external energy supplies or by constraints to free trade
- one can easily find proposals for fighting these global challenges with **combined forces:** an example from the text is Blair's suggestion that there should be a follow-up agreement to the Kyoto protocol
- another effect of combining forces could be that the UN's potential for action could be strengthened and broadened; besides, the G8 summit could and should become a powerful instrument for framing aims of mutual interest
- still one must consider **different perspectives** from Blair's thesis:
  - on a personal level we all could do our daily share: for example fighting poverty by buying fair-trade products; we can also help save the climate by saving energy (e. g. using public transport more frequently, switching off electronic devices after use)
  - the implications for industrial nations go further: there would have to be contracts that ensure for example fair trade conditions or meeting environmental standards - both of which would have negative effects on short term cost-effectiveness; that means that there must be a compromise between the short-term financial interest of the nations and the global challenges which influence individual nations in the long run
- one could also ask whether the common grounds which the wealthy nations share, e. g. the set of values like freedom, democracy and justice, are really dependably safe
- one could argue that definitions of freedom and democracy are quite often influenced by economic interests; some argue that the USA's mission to bring freedom to Iraq has been strongly influenced by Iraq's possession of oil fields

3.2 Re-creation of text: After Tony Blair's speech ... Write the speech.

HINWEIS In dieser Aufgabe sollen Sie sich selbst mit der Textsorte *political speech* kreativ auseinandersetzen und eine fiktive Antwortrede eines indischen Politikers auf Blairs Rede formulieren.

Lösungsschritte zu Aufgabe 3.2

1	Beachten Sie die verwendeten Operatoren (hier: *write the speech*).
2	Nutzen Sie Ihre Aufzeichnungen zu den vorherigen Aufgaben, um noch einmal Blairs Kernaussagen zu betrachten.
3	Rekapitulieren Sie die politische und wirtschaftliche Situation Indiens und seine besondere Beziehung zu Großbritannien.
4	Überlegen Sie, auf welche Aussagen der indische Politiker Bezug nehmen würde und welche Position er einnehmen würde.
5	Formulieren Sie eine zentrale These für Ihre Rede.
6	Formulieren Sie darüber hinaus, welches Ziel die Rede erreichen soll, vor welchem Publikum sie gehalten wird und welchen *tone* und *register* Sie wählen möchten.
7	Wählen Sie bestimmte *rhetoric devices,* um die Aufmerksamkeit der Hörer zu erlangen oder um bestimmte Thesen deutlicher zu formulieren bzw. zu überspitzen.
8	Beachten Sie die Strukturelemente einer Rede: *introduction, body, conclusion.*

Stichpunktlösung zu Aufgabe 3.2

The speaker introduces himself.	■ political function ■ reason for invitation ■ relationship to Tony Blair and Great Britain
The speaker directly or indirectly refers to specific passages of Blair's speech.	*[...] Mr. Blair has put forward the thesis that "self interest and mutual interest are inextricably linked". And I can only say: What, if not this statement, can overcome the hesitant states who still try to ignore the pressing need for action? [...]*
The perspective of the Indian politician is taken throughout the whole speech.	■ postulating political interests of India ■ commenting on the special (historical and current) connection between India and Great Britain ■ possible criticism is uttered very politely
The speaker comments on Blair's statements with reference to his background knowledge of India.	*[...] Mr. Blair, you have asked India, Japan, the US and Europe to join forces and to create a network to take us beyond 2012, to save our environment. To this I can fully agree. Still, our government holds the opinion that curbing emissions should primarily be the responsibility of those states that have largely caused them. We do not want to shirk our duties; at the same time we are sure the other states do take* ***their*** *duties seriously and do not want others to atone for mistakes they have not made in the past. [...]*

Schnell-Check zu Aufgabe II

Auf-gabe	Thema/Aufgabentyp			Trainingstipps
1	*Outline* ... Im Text dargestellte Sachverhalte kurz umreißen			■ Üben Sie, einen Text nach relevanten Informationen zu scannen. ■ Wiederholen Sie die Kriterien zum Verfassen einer *summary*. ■ Schlagen Sie themenrelevantes Vokabular nach, um sich sprachlich vorzubereiten. ■ Wiederholen Sie Konnektoren, um Ihren Text logisch zu strukturieren.
2	*Explain* ... Etwas erläutern oder erklären			■ Wiederholen Sie das entsprechende Fachvokabular für folgende Bereiche: *rhetorical devices, components/ structure of a speech.* ■ Formulieren Sie probehalber *para-graphs,* in denen Sie z. B. erläutern, zu welchen Annahmen Blair sein Publikum durch den Gebrauch von Aufzählungen *(enumerations)* zu beeinflussen versucht. ■ Wiederholen Sie die Kriterien zum Verfassen eines Essays. ■ Üben Sie das Formulieren von *paragraphs.*

Aufgabe	Thema/Aufgabentyp	☺	☹	Trainingstipps
3.1	*Comment on ...* Eine im Text vorkommende Aussage kommentieren			■ Wiederholen Sie Kernbegriffe und Vokabular des Themenbereiches. ■ Lesen Sie die Aufgabenstellung sorgfältig und notieren Sie, welche Teilbereiche Sie kommentieren und erläutern müssen. Ordnen Sie diesen jeweils aussagekräftige Argumente sowohl aus dem Text als auch aus Ihrem persönlichen Hintergrundwissen zu. ■ Beachten Sie bei Ihrer Arbeit die einzunehmende Perspektive im *comment*. ■ Üben Sie, diese vielfältigen Aspekte in Ihrem Essay in eine sinnvolle Reihenfolge zu bringen. Dabei kann eine Strukturlegetechnik sehr hilfreich sein. Hierzu notieren Sie Ihre Ergebnisse auf Kärtchen und *clustern* diese. ■ Nach der Strukturierung Ihrer Ergebnisse können Sie Ihre These zur Fragestellung formulieren, in der Sie ein Statement zu seiner Forderung abgeben. ■ Üben Sie auch die Formulierung einer Conclusio.
3.2	*Write a speech.* Eine Rede schreiben			■ Wiederholen Sie Kernbegriffe und Vokabular des Themenbereiches. ■ Lesen Sie die Aufgabenstellung sorgfältig und notieren Sie, welche Teilaspekte Sie beachten müssen. ■ Beachten Sie bei Ihrer Arbeit die einzunehmende Perspektive. ■ Wiederholen Sie Aufbau und typische Ziele einer *political speech.* ■ Üben Sie, eine sprachlich angemessene und interessante Rede zu formulieren und sich dabei in sinnvoller Weise rhetorischer Figuren zu bedienen. ■ Üben Sie auch die Formulierung einer Conclusio.

PRÜFUNGSAUFGABEN 2009

Aufgabentyp	Textaufgabe: comprehension, analysis, evaluation
Thema/ Schwerpunkt	British and American traditions and visions: The American Dream then and now Globalization – global challenges: Economic and ecological issues
Material	Joyce Carol Oates: Dreaming America
Textsorte	Literarischer Text: Gedicht

Aufgabe I

Aufgabenstellung:

1 Describe the process of American civilization and the reactions to it as presented in the poem. **(Comprehension) (16 Punkte)**

2 Analyse the speaker's attitude to this process of civilization. Focus on the poem's structure, language and stylistic devices. **(Analysis) (24 Punkte)**

3 Choose <u>one</u> of the following tasks:

3.1 Comment on Oates' poem as a statement on the American Dream. **(Evaluation: comment) (20 Punkte)**

3.2 Imagine you are the thirteen-year-old girl *"dreaming into the window of Levitz's Record Shop"* (ll. 35 – 36). Write down the girl's dreams and thoughts in the form of an interior monologue. The title should be *"My American Dream"*. **(Evaluation: re-creation of text) (20 Punkte)**

Text

Joyce Carol Oates
Dreaming America

When the two-lane highway was widened
the animals retreated.
Skunks, raccoons, rabbits - even their small corpses
disappeared from the road - transformed into rags
then into designs
then into stains
then nothing.

When the highway was linked to another
then to another
six lanes then nine then twelve rose
sweeping to the horizon
along measured white lines.
The polled Herefords were sold.
When the cornfields were bulldozed
the farmhouses at their edges turned into shanties;
the outbuildings fell.

When the fields were paved over
Frisch's Big Boy rose seventy-five feet in the air.
The *Sunoco* and *Texaco* and *Gulf* signs competed
on hundred-foot stilts
like eyeballs on stalks
white optic-nerves
miraculous.
Illuminated at night.

Where the useless stretch of trees lay
an orange sphere like a golf ball
announces the Shopping Mall, open
for Thursday evening shopping.
There, tonight, droves of teenagers hunt
one another, alert on the memorized pavement.

Where did the country go? - cry the travelers, soaring
past. *Where did the country go?* - ask the strangers.
The teenagers never ask.

Where horses grazed in a dream that had no history,
tonight a thirteen-year-old girl stands dreaming
into the window of Levitz's Record Shop.
We drive past, in a hurry. We disappear.
We return.

210 words

Joyce Carol Oates: Dreaming America (1975). In: The Fabulous Beasts, Poems by Joyce Carol Oates, Baton Rouge; London: Louisiana State University Press, 1975, S. 83 - 84

Annotations

13 The polled Herefords: breed of beef cattle with horns cut
18 Frisch's Big Boy: chain of family-style restaurants
19 Sunoco, Texaco, Gulf signs: gas stations owned by the respective companies

Aufgabentyp	Textaufgabe: comprehension, analysis, evaluation
Thema/ Schwerpunkt	British and American traditions and visions: British history: From Empire to Commonwealth, monarchy and modern democracy, the UK and Europe Globalization - global challenges: International peace-keeping at the turn of the century: the role of the UN and the USA
Material	Heather Brooke: Has anybody in Britain actually read '1984'? In: The Independent
Textsorte	Sach- und Gebrauchstext: Kommentar der internationalen Presse

Aufgabe II

Aufgabenstellung:

1 Outline Heather Brooke's view on Britain's security policies, on the public's reactions, and on the action that should be taken by the readers.

(Comprehension) (16 Punkte)

2 Examine the way Brooke tries to convince and mobilize the reader. Focus on her line of argumentation and use of language. **(Analysis) (24 Punkte)**

3 Choose <u>one</u> of the following tasks:

3.1 "Constant surveillance, files on innocent people, secret trials - these are the hallmarks of a police state [...]" (ll. 33 - 34). Discuss to what extent a citizen in a globalized world has to accept living under certain restrictions for the sake of security. Give an evaluation of the author's position.

(Evaluation: comment) (20 Punkte)

3.2 You are from Tunbridge Wells (cf. l. 17). Write a letter to the editor in which you strongly oppose Brooke's reproaches to the British public as well as her misjudgement of the political situation in the UK.

(Evaluation: re-creation of text) (20 Punkte)

Text

Heather Brooke, "Has anybody in Britain actually read '1984'?"

The Independent, 13 October 2005

"There was, of course, no way of knowing whether you were being watched at any given moment. How often, or on what system, the Thought Police plugged in on any individual wire was guesswork. It was even conceivable that they watched everybody all the time."

George Orwell, *1984*

It seems appropriate that the author of *1984* was a British citizen. George Orwell must have seen how easily the great British public's lamb-like disposition toward its leaders could be exploited to create a police state. Say what you will about Americans, but one thing they are not is passive. The Bush administration may have pushed through the Patriot Act weeks after 11 September, but, as the American public got to grips with how the law was affecting their individual rights, their protests grew loud and angry.

Yesterday saw the publication of the Government's latest Anti-terror Bill that would give police even more power. The House of Lords, meanwhile, is debating the Racial and Religious Hatred Bill, and Whitehall is investigating ways to ban former civil servants from publishing their accounts of what happens in the corridors of power.

There are already nearly 200 pieces of anti-terrorism legislation. What else can be left except thought-crime? The police and politicians have scented power and they want to run it to ground. The Metropolitan Police Commissioner Sir Ian Blair shamelessly demands more laws even while his department is under investigation for shooting dead an innocent Brazilian.

But never underestimate the British public's lack of interest in serious issues. They may moan and gripe, but the most they are likely to do is to write a letter to the editor, "Yours outraged, Tunbridge Wells". Soon enough, they will be back gobbling up their junk diet of celebrity piffle.

[...]

Meanwhile, the public is being banned from protesting within 1 km of Parliament. The Serious Crime and Police Powers Act makes it a criminal offence to trespass on a "designated site" for "national security" reasons. It is likely we'll see the law used against protesters. Police can also store a person's details, fingerprints and DNA when that person is arrested. You don't have to be found guilty for the police to swab your mouth and keep records on you; simply looking suspicious or being in the wrong place at the wrong time is reason enough.

I hopped on a London bus recently and found my face broadcast on both decks. The cameras are to make us feel safer. They make me feel violated. I'd feel safer if the police were more accountable and told me, for example, how many officers patrol my neighbourhood or the number of times police fail to show up when called.

Across government, institutional privacy is protected at all costs, while individual privacy is under assault. Yet the passive faces of my bus companions show a society so dulled into submission they resemble stunned cows lined up for slaughter. I can't help thinking that in America there would be petitions, leaflets, protests, maybe even armed violence.

Constant surveillance, files on innocent people, secret trials - these are the hallmarks of a police state, one that is being erected with the meek acceptance of the British public.

Where are the fighters in the UK? Where is the concern that the state is invading every single nook of our privacy? That the police are becoming more politicised and more powerful? That politicians are cloaking themselves in secrecy under the guise of national security for the most ridiculous of reasons.

What should happen is this - we should give no more power to the state without the state giving something to us. If the Government wants to keep a database of our identities, then it should publish its entire staff directory so we can see who is doing what at taxpayers' expense. If the police want to detain people for longer periods, they must tell us who these people are and what they are accused of doing; they must provide enough evidence to a judge to warrant such internment.

Here's what you can do: write to your MP or send a fax or an email to them via www.writetothem.com. See what they say on anti-terror laws or ID cards at www.theyworkforyou.com, attend a local council meeting, start asking questions and demand accountability from all those public bodies who take your money. You could even form a citizens' group or donate money to an existing pro-democracy campaign such as Liberty, Justice, Inquest, www.Mysociety.org. The alternative is real life Big Brother with all the grainy grimness of a CCTV photo shoot.

777 words

Heather Brooke: Has anybody in Britain actually read '1984'? In: The Independent, 13 October 2005

Annotations

1984:	dystopian novel in which the citizens are constantly watched through special monitors by *Big Brother,* i. e. by the state, seeking to prevent the citizens from committing "thought-crime"
4	Patriot Act: an American law allowing the interception of phone calls
9	Whitehall: seat of the British government in London
12 - 13:	to run it to ground (metaphorical usage): *here:* to gain control without a democratic mandate
14:	the Brazilian referred to in this line was suspected to be a terrorist and shot dead by the police; it turned out, however, that he had been an innocent member of the public
17	Tunbridge Wells: provincial town in Kent
17	piffle: *(infml.)* nonsense
50	CCTV: abbreviation for closed circuit television

LÖSUNGSVORSCHLAG 2009

Aufgabe I

1 Comprehension: Describe the process of American civilization ...

HINWEIS In dieser Aufgabe sollen Sie den Prozess der amerikanischen Zivilisation und die Reaktionen darauf beschreiben, so wie sie im Gedicht dargestellt werden.

Lösungsschritte zu Aufgabe 1

1	Prüfen Sie die verwendeten Operatoren. Diese geben Ihnen genaue Informationen darüber, was Sie in der Aufgabe zu leisten haben (hier: *describe*).
2	Scannen Sie das Gedicht gezielt nach Informationen zu den zu untersuchenden Aspekten: *process of civilization* und *reactions to it.* Markieren Sie diese entweder farbig im Text oder notieren Sie sie tabellarisch.
3	Benennen Sie Autor, Titel, Textart und Entstehungsjahr in Ihrem Einleitungssatz.
4	Lösen Sie sich vom Text und formulieren Sie eine kurze Zusammenfassung in eigenen Worten. Denken Sie an die Verwendung des *Simple Present* und von Konnektoren, damit die logischen Zusammenhänge deutlich werden.
5	Vermeiden Sie in diesem Aufgabenbereich Kommentare, persönliche Wertungen oder Analysen.
6	Beachten Sie, dass Sie weder wörtliche Rede noch Zitate verwenden dürfen.
7	Strukturieren Sie Ihren Text in *paragraphs,* welche jeweils nur einen Aspekt beinhalten sollten.

Stichpunktlösung zu Aufgabe 1

Process of civilization:

- this process is divided into **different phases:** at first the natural environment of several species is destroyed completely, then a new infrastructure is built, finally the whole country is encompassed by urban development
- expanding the infrastructure destroys the habitat of indigenous species and the meadowland by linking highways or bulldozing cornfields; the dying of the species is illustrated by the carcasses of animals fringing the highways
- these landscapes are then taken over by big concerns, which erect huge statues of advertising characters for fast-food chains, illuminated billboards for oil companies and shopping malls

Reactions to it:

- different groups of people react in different ways to these changes: travelers and strangers ask about the past and the present of the country; they arrive, they leave again and then return with their questions
- the teenagers in the shopping malls do not ask any questions; they live and dream only in the here and now

2 Analysis: Analyse the speaker's attitude to ... Focus on ...

HINWEIS Sie sollen in dieser Aufgabe analysieren, mit welchen sprachlichen und rhetorischen Mitteln der Sprecher seine Einstellung zum *process of civilisation* ausdrückt. Dabei sollen insbesondere *structure, language* und *stylistic devices* untersucht werden.

NÜTZLICHE WENDUNGEN **Operator *analyse***

- to illustrate s.th.
- to exemplify s.th.
- to be an expression of/for s.th.
- to stand for s.th.
- an expression for s.th.
- to express s.th.
- to establish s.th.
- to be a sign for s.th.

Lösungsschritte zu Aufgabe 2

1	Prüfen Sie die verwendeten Operatoren. Diese geben Ihnen genaue Informationen darüber, was Sie in der Aufgabe zu leisten haben (hier: *analyse*).
2	Scannen Sie den Text und Ihre Aufzeichnungen nach Informationen und Vokabular zu den geforderten Bereichen: *structure of a poem (stanza, verse, rhyme scheme, metre), stylistic devices (metaphor, anaphora, personification, rhetorical question, simile, irony ...), language (sentence structure, tone, register, active voice/passive voice ...)* und benennen Sie, was Ihnen darüber hinaus noch auffällt.
3	Unterstreichen oder notieren Sie aussagekräftige Beispiele.
4	Formulieren Sie einen Einleitungssatz, in dem Sie thesenartig die Meinung des Sprechers zum *process of civilization* proklamieren.
5	Erläutern Sie jeweils auch die **Funktion** und **Wirkung** der von Ihnen analysierten Aspekte.
6	Strukturieren Sie Ihren Text in *paragraphs*, welche jeweils nur einen Aspekt beinhalten sollten.
7	Vergessen Sie nicht, am Ende eine zusammenfassende Conclusio zu formulieren.

Stichpunktlösung zu Aufgabe 2

Introduction:

- the attitude of the speaker is critical; this is manifest in the structure of the poem, its language and the stylistic devices used

Structure of the poem/language:

- **structure of the poem:** each stanza expresses the gradual changing of the American landscape and the American set of values for the worse
- **structure of the sentences:** the aspect that is changed is always expressed by an adverbial clause in the first verse of each stanza ("When the two-lane-highway was widened the animals retreated.")
- **textual coherence** is established by the 13-year-old girl who "stands" actually "dreaming" (as the title *Dreaming America* suggests) an (American) Dream
- the question "Where did the country go?" is the **culmination** of the aforementioned development of America

Stylistic devices:

- the continual threat to the country finally leads to a loss of natural resources for living creatures; this is illustrated by the use of stylistic devices, for example **nouns which refer to the disappearance of things** ("corpses", "rags", "designs", "stains", "nothing")
- there is also **irony** used when referring to the "useless stretch of trees"
- the **rhetorical question** "Where did the country go?" also expresses the loss of an essential piece of the original America
- nature has been replaced by anonymous and artificial powers that dominate and manipulate human beings
- this is exemplified by the use of **personifications** like "signs competed", "six lanes ... rose", "an orange sphere ... announces the Shopping Mall" and **similes** ("like eyeballs on stalks", "an orange sphere like a golf ball")
- the use of the **passive voice** illustrates the artificial power that now persists in the world: "was widened", "was linked", "were sold", "were bulldozed"

Other: the American Dream – an interpretation

- the example of the thirteen-year-old girl can be understood as a double reference to the American Dream:
- on the one hand, the girl stands for the **materialistic interpretation** of the American Dream, i. e. she is one of the "droves of teenagers" **(metaphor)** whose only concern and dreams are the goods on display in the shopping malls and who takes the situation for granted
- at the same time she is presented as an individual who is (still) able to dream, who pauses for a moment and thereby fits into the reflexive tenor of the poem; this could be seen as a **new and individual interpretation** of the American Dream

NÜTZLICHE WENDUNGEN **Stilmittel/stylistic devices**

- verse
- stanza
- poem
- speaker
- simile
- personification
- enumeration
- passive voice
- textual coherence
- metaphor
- rhetorical question
- rhyme scheme
- metre
- simile
- irony

3.1 Comment: Comment on Oates' poem as a statement ...

HINWEIS In dieser Aufgabe sollen Sie Oates' Gedicht unter der Fragestellung kommentieren, welches Statement sie darin zum *American Dream* abgibt.

Lösungsschritte zu Aufgabe 3.1

1	Prüfen Sie die verwendeten Operatoren und Hinweise. Diese geben Ihnen genaue Informationen darüber, was Sie in der Aufgabe zu leisten haben (hier: *comment on*).
2	Scannen Sie das Gedicht und Ihre Aufzeichnungen kurz nach Informationen zu den relevanten Teilaspekten (Bezugspunkte zum *American Dream*) und überlegen Sie, woran Sie sich zusätzlich aus den durchgeführten Unterrichtsreihen erinnern: *Manifest Destiny, progress, challenges, frontier, dream vs. nightmare, a better life.*
3	Unterstreichen oder notieren Sie aussagekräftige Passagen.
4	Machen Sie sich Ihre persönliche Einstellung zu diesem Thema deutlich und formulieren Sie diese klar und anschaulich.
5	Formulieren Sie einen Einleitungssatz, in dem Sie eine erste These zu Oates' Einstellung zum *American Dream* anführen.
6	Bauen Sie Ihren Essay sachlogisch auf und verbinden Sie Ihre Gedankengänge mit passenden Konnektoren.
7	Benennen Sie jeweils passende Belege und Beispiele zur Untermauerung Ihrer Ausführungen.
8	Strukturieren Sie Ihren Text in *paragraphs,* welche jeweils nur einen Aspekt beinhalten sollten.
9	Vergessen Sie nicht, am Ende eine zusammenfassende Conclusio zu formulieren.

Ausführlicher Lösungsvorschlag zu Aufgabe 3.1

Oates sees the materialistic interpretation of the American Dream critically, with which I must partly agree.

The American Dream has been the shared dream of many who came to the new world and wanted to start over. They believed in principles like Manifest Destiny, progress, challenges and overcoming ever new frontiers.
But this dream very often turns into a nightmare. The chance of making one's dream come true is a matter of luck, today even more than in the times of the settlers. Then, America

really was a country in which white settlers had a lot to explore, a country to form according to their ideas, where they could hope to gain personal and religious freedom.
These dreams were fulfilled at the cost of many: the indigenous tribes were slowly but steadily corralled, nature was fought back and many dreams ended before they began.
Today nature seems to be excluded from the modern Dream. There is nearly no trace left of the country that was the land of dreams of so many. It has become a strange country, filled with short-lived embodiments of commercialized dreams. These dreams are shown in the shop windows of modern cities, in the skylines, where big telescreens broadcast the latest Dream (everything needs to be bigger, better and faster) and even in the faces of celebrities - those role models for the dreams of the average consumer. Young, attractive, healthy, sexy, intelligent and successful - these adjectives encompass the Dream of today's society.
It is not only teenagers who are attracted to the enchanting staging of a life in which everything is possible - like in shows such as "American Idol". We all want to have it all, but without the effort our forefathers thought to be essential to the American Dream.

Alas, there are different aspects to the Dream, besides the mere materialistic aspect as symbolized by the teenagers in the poem. Equal opportunity is established by law in the USA, the relative standard of education is high. If you try hard you can win scholarships and escape from poor neighborhoods. The standard of living of many does include small luxuries like cars, TVs, computers, a fully furnished apartment ... But one still has to work hard to first achieve and then maintain this standard. The support by the state for the poor, for example as far as the health system is concerned, is not as all-encompassing as in Germany. If you do not have health insurance you might not be treated in time.

Oates' poem strongly contrasts the old way of living (farming, herding ...) to the modern one (cities, shopping malls) and she appears to be in favour of the first. I am not sure that she is not idealizing the past. In the examples I mentioned it has always been a matter of luck and personal involvement for your dream to come true. The dreams have changed, what still exists is the notion that it really is possible to achieve your goals and that the USA is a good place for it. And there is hope left after all: the girl is still able to dream; she is presented as an individual, which illustrates that not all people are drowning in the masses of easily entertained and unthinking consumers; even the spectators (i. e. we) return after their first unthinking passing to stop for a while and reflect.

(563 words)

3.2 Re-creation of text: Imagine you are ... Write down the girl's dreams ...

HINWEIS In dieser Aufgabe sind Sie gebeten, in einem *interior monologue* die Träume und Gedanken des 13-jährigen Mädchens, das die Schaufensterauslagen träumend betrachtet, darzustellen. Zu diesem Zweck müssen Sie dessen Perspektive erarbeiten und eine sach- und altersgemäße Darstellungsform in der Ich-Perspektive wählen.

Lösungsschritte zu Aufgabe 3.2

1	Prüfen Sie die verwendeten Operatoren und Hinweise. Diese geben Ihnen genaue Informationen darüber, was Sie in der Aufgabe zu leisten haben (hier: ... *in the form of an interior monologue ... title should be "My American Dream"*).
2	Scannen Sie den Text und Ihre Aufzeichnungen kurz nach Informationen zu den relevanten Teilaspekten: *presentation of aspects of the American Dream (freedom, frontier, from rags to riches ...).*
3	Beachten Sie, dass aus der Perspektive einer Dreizehnjährigen diese Elemente keinen abstrakten, sondern einen konkreten, greifbaren Charakter haben müssen. Es müssen realistische Wünsche, Träume, Ängste sein, die sich auf die Lebenswirklichkeit des Mädchens beziehen.
4	Achten Sie auch bei Ihren Formulierungen darauf, dass sie zum Sprachgebrauch eines Teenagers passen müssen. Beispiel: Verwenden Sie **nicht** die Ihnen geläufigen Fachtermini, sondern umschreiben Sie sie konkret.

Stichpunktlösung zu Aufgabe 3.2

Writing from the girl's perspective:

- she might dream of age-appropriate things like fashion as a means of expressing one's personality, not having to argue with her parents about things she desires like the time she has to be back home, the people with whom she spends her time, the amount of pocket money she receives, the music/stars she chooses for their message/charisma (freedom) → American Dream, partly materialistic interpretation
- she might also be afraid of the world she is living in (being portrayed as the dreaming and reflecting individual among all the others who do not think), she might for example be aware of the destruction of the environment and fear for her future, she might also know about a high unemployment rate, the big gap between poor and rich, the difficulty of affording a good education if you are poor → American Nightmare

Linking the content of the poem with own ideas and background knowledge:

- "sweeping to the horizon": frontier → there are no limits to progress, there is hardly any wildlife left in some areas
- "tonight, droves of teenagers hunt one another"; "tonight a thirteen-year-old girl stands dreaming": people have replaced nature, they dream a new dream that is full of neon signs, people, consumption – or they dream themselves back into a time when the "farmhouses", "skunks, raccoons, rabbits" and "cornfields" still exist

Possible result of analysis:

- the girl might be torn between two opposing forces: on the one hand she is part of the group of teenagers who do not ask "where did the country go?" and who hunt one another in the shopping malls, on the other hand she is able to stop for a little while and dream (and possibly reflect her situation)

Things the girl might dream about:

- fashion or goods on display, freedom, return to nature, wish to protect the environment, friendship

HINWEIS Am Ende sollten Sie einen logischen Abschluss finden, z. B. eine Unterbrechung durch eine andere Person oder eine Entscheidung, die das Mädchen am Ende fällt.

Ausführlicher Lösungsvorschlag zu Aufgabe 3.2

My American Dream

I wish I had more money left and hadn't bought that LP last month. I can't even afford to buy a single record. And now everyone owns the latest single from La Belle, everyone but me. Money ... it's all about money. Is it my fault that my mom doesn't earn so much? Is it my fault that Dad hasn't got a job? The girls at school just care about their clothes. "See you at the mall!" – that's all they're interested in. And I go here on my own and look at the displays and into the store windows and dream about all the things I would buy if I ever had enough money. None of the girls invite me to join them. They must think I'm a weirdo because I never have any cool clothes, records or the newest hairdo. I hate arguing with my dad about these things. He always says I am a material girl (whatever that means) and that I should be happy to have all the things I possess and that I can get a decent education. Decent education! That's ok for the future – but I am living here and now. And just now I'd rather be like the others.

That's Cindy and Sandy over there, carrying their mom's shopping from the little vegetable store around the corner. They're different from all the others and they always talk to me. They moved here from the country just six months ago. They don't have much money either. Their

dad had to sell the farm because some oil company bought all the land and he was the only farmer left in this area. And they needed his land for a new highway.
Sandy says the highways are killing all the animals, at least those we have not killed yet for their furs. I wonder if we really kill so many animals for their fur?
Still, I like the highways. I like it when mom and I go to Detroit by bus before Christmas and I can see everything rushing by through the windows. Oh, and I love the shopping mall in Detroit. I can pick one thing I'd like to have for Christmas - unless it's more than 20 dollars - and we always have lunch at a big fast food restaurant! That's the life I'd like to live when I'm grown up: shopping, eating out, going on trips - feeling free and being able to do anything I want to do.
Cindy says they never eat fast food. She says her dad told them it's unhealthy and the chains destroy the businesses of small restaurants. She says it's the big chains' fault that Mrs. Miller from across the street had to close her nice little restaurant where you could get the nicest and crispiest fries. I like Mrs. Miller - and her fries. And I feel sorry that she and her son have to live on unemployment money now. I remember how bad it was when we had to live on it.

I wonder if Cindy is right. She doesn't like the city very much. And she says we're thoughtless. We COULD improve some things if we only tried: save the environment, live healthy. She says we are too obsessed with things and care too little about important issues like friendship. She says her dream would be to change our country for the better.
Sure, some changes would be nice. And what she says does sound interesting and plausible. Still, I don't quite know what she means by all this ... I'll ask her about it tomorrow at school.

(612 words)

Schnell-Check zu Aufgabe I

Auf- gabe	Thema/Aufgabentyp			Trainingstipps
1	*Describe ...* Einen im Text dargestellten Sachverhalt beschreiben			■ Üben Sie, einen Text nach relevanten Informationen zu scannen. ■ Wiederholen Sie die Kriterien zum Verfassen einer *summary*. ■ Schlagen Sie themenrelevantes Vokabular nach, um sich sprachlich vorzubereiten. ■ Wiederholen Sie Konnektoren, um Ihren Text logisch zu strukturieren.
2	*Analyse ...* Die Einstellung des Sprechers analysieren			■ Wiederholen Sie das entsprechende Fachvokabular für folgende Bereiche: *structure, language* und *stylistic devices.* ■ Üben Sie Formulierungen, in denen Sie z. B. die Struktur des Gedichtes beschreiben und ihre Wirkung auf den Leser erläutern. ■ Wiederholen Sie die Kriterien zum Verfassen eines Essays. ■ Üben Sie das Formulieren von *paragraphs.*

Aufgabe	Thema/Aufgabentyp			Trainingstipps
3.1	*Comment on ...* Eine Aussage des Textes kommentieren			■ Sehen Sie Ihre Unterlagen durch und erstellen Sie Begriffsnetze oder Mindmaps, um Ihr Wissen und Ihren Lernstoff zu vernetzen. ■ Üben Sie, die verschiedenen Einzelbereiche in einer sinnvollen Reihenfolge zu verknüpfen, sodass die einzelnen *paragraphs* sachlogisch aufeinander aufbauen. ■ Wiederholen Sie die Kriterien zum Verfassen eines Essays. ■ Schlagen Sie themenrelevantes Vokabular nach, um sich sprachlich vorzubereiten.
3.2	*Write ... an interior monologue ...* Einen inneren Monolog schreiben			■ Üben Sie, *interior monologues* zu verfassen. ■ Schlagen Sie themenrelevantes Vokabular nach, um sich sprachlich vorzubereiten. ■ Üben Sie das Formulieren von *paragraphs,* falls Sie sich entschieden haben, der Dreizehnjährigen einen eher sachlogisch orientierten Gedankenprozess zuzuschreiben. Alternativ können Sie auch trainieren, den *stream of consciousness* (eine teilweise unstrukturierte Aufeinanderfolge von verschiedenen Gedankenprozessen) darzustellen.

Aufgabe II

1 Comprehension: Outline Heather Brooke's view on ...

HINWEIS In der ersten Aufgabe sollen Sie Heather Brookes Meinung zu Großbritanniens Außen- und Sicherheitspolitik wiedergeben. Zudem müssen Sie die tatsächlichen öffentlichen Reaktionen auf diese Politik und die Reaktionen, die Brooke von den Lesern eigentlich erwartet und fordert, anführen.

Lösungsschritte zu Aufgabe 1

1	Prüfen Sie die verwendeten Operatoren. Diese geben Ihnen genaue Informationen darüber, was Sie in der Aufgabe zu leisten haben (hier: *outline*).
2	Scannen Sie den Text gezielt nach Informationen zu den Themenbereichen *Britain's security policy, public reaction* und *expected reactions.* Markieren Sie diese entweder farbig im Text oder notieren Sie sie tabellarisch.
3	Benennen Sie Autor, Titel, Textart und Entstehungsjahr in Ihrem Einleitungssatz.
4	Lösen Sie sich vom Text und formulieren Sie eine kurze Zusammenfassung in eigenen Worten. Denken Sie an die Verwendung des *Simple Present* und von Konnektoren, damit die logischen Zusammenhänge deutlich werden.
6	Vermeiden Sie in diesem Aufgabenbereich Kommentare, persönliche Wertungen oder Analysen.
7	Beachten Sie, dass Sie weder wörtliche Rede noch Zitate verwenden dürfen.
8	Strukturieren Sie Ihren Text in *paragraphs,* welche jeweils nur einen Aspekt beinhalten sollten.

Stichpunktlösung zu Aufgabe 1

Britain's security policy:

- Brooke sees Britain's security policy critically
- she points out that there is a tendency to create a surveillance society, in which civil liberty is reduced; this is reminiscent of the situation in Orwell's novel *1984*
- according to Brooke the reasons for the limitations on civil liberty and the increasing surveillance of citizens are based on the fear for national security after numerous terrorist attacks

- in this context she criticizes the (too) high number of already passed anti-terrorism laws, the geographical limitation of protester's rights and the storage of personal data of "suspects"
- she considers the politicians' and the police's striving for power to be another reason for the current development; her examples to support her thesis are that the police are permitted to monitor and to arrest people without court order, that the police are generally given too much influence and that politicians can exert more and more control, allegedly in order to maintain national security

Reactions to it/expected reactions:

- whereas the British population appears to be impartial to this development, Brooke insists that the initiative of every single citizen is important in order to retain civil liberty
- means that could be taken are for example forming a citizens' group, starting a dialogue with politicians or donating money to pro-democracy campaigns like Liberty, Justice or Inquest

2 Analysis: Examine the way Brooke tries to convince ...

HINWEIS In dieser Aufgabe sollen Sie untersuchen, auf welche Weise Heather Brooke versucht, ihre Leserschaft von ihrer Auffassung zu überzeugen und zum Handeln zu mobilisieren. In diesem Zusammenhang liegen die Untersuchungsschwerpunkte auf der Argumentationsstruktur des Textes und dem Sprachgebrauch der Autorin.

Lösungsschritte zu Aufgabe 2

1	Prüfen Sie die verwendeten Operatoren. Diese geben Ihnen genaue Informationen darüber, was Sie in der Aufgabe zu leisten haben (hier: *examine*).
2	Scannen Sie den Text und Ihre Aufzeichnungen nach Informationen und Vokabular zu den geforderten Bereichen: *line of argumentation, language* (hier: *irony, inclusive we, professional terminology [„legalese"], colloquialisms, black humour, use of contrasts, repetitive use of modal auxilliaries and imperatives*) und benennen Sie, was Ihnen darüber hinaus noch auffällt.
3	Unterstreichen oder notieren Sie aussagekräftige Beispiele.

4	Formulieren Sie einen Einleitungssatz, in dem Sie thesenartig die Meinung Brookes zu *Britain's security policy* proklamieren. Ergänzen Sie diesen durch einen Hinweis auf Ihre Arbeitshypothese. Dazu können Sie sprachliche Elemente aus der Aufgabenstellung nutzen: *Brooke tries to convince her readers that it is time to take action against state surveillance. To show how she tries to reach her aims, I am going to examine her line of argumentation and also focus on her use of language.*
5	Untersuchen Sie den Textauszug bezüglich Argumentationsstruktur und Sprachgebrauch und markieren Sie entsprechende Passagen farbig.
6	Erstellen Sie eine Grobstruktur für Ihren Essay, welche Sie entweder aspektorientiert oder chronologisch an den Textverlauf angelegt gestalten können. Falls Sie sich für eine Gliederung nach inhaltlichen Aspekten entscheiden (vgl. Lösungsvorschlag), umgehen Sie so die ansonsten üblichen Wiederholungen von Punkten, die bereits in vorherigen *paragraphs* genannt wurden.
7	Benennen Sie jeweils **Funktion** und **Wirkung** der von Ihnen aufgeführten Beispiele.
8	Strukturieren Sie Ihren Text insgesamt in *paragraphs,* welche jeweils nur einen Aspekt beinhalten sollten.
9	Vergessen Sie nicht, am Ende eine zusammenfassende Conclusio zu formulieren.

Stichpunktlösung zu Aufgabe 2

Introduction:

- the attitude of the speaker is critical; this is manifest in the structure of the poem, its language and the stylistic devices used

Referring to George Orwell's dystopian novel *1984* as a warning of future consequences:

- the headline and the quote at the beginning are supposed to rouse and at the same time scare the readers
- they are expected to see parallels between the society in the novel and their own society ("being watched at any given moment"; "What else can be left except thought-crime?")
- the final reference to "Big Brother" appears to be a warning about what might happen if citizens do not exercise their political rights

Pointing out ways in which Britain is showing signs of developing into a police state to make the British population aware of the potential dangers:

- one example is the fact that there are "nearly 200 pieces of anti-terrorism legislation" and there are even more bills being discussed every day ("latest Anti-terror Bill that would give police even more power"; "debating the Racial and Religious Hatred

Bill"; "investigating ways to ban former civil servants from publishing their accounts of what happens in the corridors of power"); the ways of interference seem to be unlimited

- her usage of juridical terminology ("criminal offence to trespass on a 'designated site' for 'national security' reasons") make her appear not only well-informed but even like an expert, which also underlines the importance of her statements
- naming Sir Ian Blair as an example for the police's and politicians' striving for power also supports her role as a well-informed judge of the situation

Criticizing the citizens' being naïve and passive in the face of the current developments:

- she ironically points out ("but the most they are likely to do") that a letter to the editor is not an adequate way of protesting
- another means to express her criticism is the use of colloquialisms like "they may moan and gripe" or "they will be back gobbling up their junk diet of celebrity piffle"; she implies that such people are shallow and passive
- she even employs examples of black humor ("a society so dulled into submission they resemble stunned cows lined up for slaughter"; "the great British public's lamb-like disposition") to assail the - in her opinion - inadequate reaction of the British to the surveillance policy

Contrasting the British public's reaction with the political self-image of the US-Americans, which she prefers to the British one:

- she describes the vehement reaction of the American society ("protests grew loud and angry") to the consequences (limitation of individual rights) of the Patriot Act; she names this as a good example of adequate political behavior in the face of unsatisfactory conditions
- she also envisions the reaction of US citizens to the camera surveillance, which she would expect to be "petitions, leaflets, protests, maybe even armed violence", whereas the British seem to show no reaction at all

Trying to arouse the British and to persuade them to protest actively:

- in her use of pronouns she clearly distinguishes between those who do nothing at all about the worsening conditions in Britain ("the great British public's lamb-like disposition towards **its** leaders"; "**They** may moan and gripe ..."; "**they** will be back gobbling ..."; "**They** [the police] must tell us ...") and those who might bring about a change; she addresses the latter group using an inclusive we ("**we** should give no more power ..."; "... so we can see ..."); in doing so she creates a sense of unity between her readership and herself to influence them in favor of her ideas

- enumerating numerous examples for political involvement provides the readers with action alternatives (for example "write to your MP"); Brooke even publishes web addresses and email addresses which readers who are interested can make use of
- in the last two paragraphs her use of modal auxiliaries ("must", "should") and imperatives support her insistent request to the British population to finally take action against the growing surveillance by the state

3.1 Comment: "Constance surveillance ..." Discuss to what extent ...

HINWEIS In diesem Essay sollen Sie sich kritisch mit der These auseinandersetzen, ob Menschen in einer globalisierten Welt nicht grundsätzlich gewisse Einschränkungen zum Schutz ihrer Sicherheit akzeptieren müssen. Dabei müssen Sie sich sowohl auf den Standpunkt von Brooke im Allgemeinen als auch auf die angegebene Textstelle beziehen.

Lösungsschritte zu Aufgabe 3.1

1	Prüfen Sie die verwendeten Operatoren und Hinweise. Diese geben Ihnen genaue Informationen darüber, was Sie in der Aufgabe zu leisten haben (hier: *discuss*).
2	Scannen Sie den Text und Ihre Aufzeichnungen kurz nach Informationen zu den relevanten Teilaspekten (Bezugspunkte zu *surveillance, citizen in a globalized world, restrictions for the sake of security*) und überlegen Sie, woran Sie sich zusätzlich aus den durchgeführten Unterrichtsreihen erinnern: *living in a globalized world, new technologies – chances and dangers, terrorism.*
3	Unterstreichen oder notieren Sie aussagekräftige Passagen.
4	Machen Sie sich Ihre persönliche Einstellung zu diesem Thema deutlich und formulieren Sie diese klar und anschaulich.
5	Formulieren Sie einen Einleitungssatz, in dem Sie eine erste These zu Brookes Standpunkt anführen.
6	Bauen Sie Ihren Essay sachlogisch auf und verbinden Sie Ihre Gedankengänge mit passenden Konnektoren.
7	Benennen Sie jeweils passende Belege und Beispiele zur Untermauerung Ihrer Ausführungen.
8	Strukturieren Sie Ihren Text in *paragraphs,* welche jeweils nur einen Aspekt beinhalten sollten.
9	Vergessen Sie nicht, am Ende eine zusammenfassende Conclusio zu formulieren.

Ausführlicher Lösungsvorschlag zu Aufgabe 3.1

I think people do have to live under certain restrictions in order to maintain their safety. Brooke's thesis that there is a surveillance society is a reaction to international terrorism in a globalized world; the increase in surveillance results from anti-terror laws, CCTV and an increase of power of police and state.

The thesis is to my mind correct insofar as for example modern forms of crime cannot be fought with old-fashioned methods of investigation; examples of felonies that people were convicted for are terrorist attacks in western countries (the Patriot Act being a result of September 11th in the USA), international forms of organized crime like child pornography which need quick and effective intervention or the attempt to reduce the number of acts of violence on buses in Great Britain by installing cameras which Brooke considered to be a violation of personal freedom.
Still one has to look at the other side of the coin: in western civilization the citizen is seen as being politically mature in a democratic society. An increase of security is not necessarily connected to a decrease of personal freedom. And finally the state is not able to protect the citizens from data abuse.
A result of the stricter policies are for example protests in the streets demanding more personal freedom. This shows that people see the new laws critically. But remembering September 11th and its implications, one must admit that we need better and more effective surveillance. And one must take it for granted that we will make mistakes on our way to a safer world – still I am convinced that what could happen if we do not act would be worse.

To put it all in a nutshell I think we must learn from history (e. g. the Nazi regime, the RAF, the observation of employees in well-known German discount stores) and try not to repeat those mistakes again. But still we must protect our safety. Brooke is right: establishing an uncontrollable surveillance state must be avoided – but not at all costs. The slogan must be safety first!

(343 words)

3.2 Re-creation of text: You are from ... Write a letter to the editor ...

> HINWEIS In dieser Aufgabe sollen Sie die Perspektive eines Bürgers aus Turnbridge Wells (vgl. Annotationen zum Klausurtext) übernehmen und einen *letter to the editor* verfassen, in welchem Sie versuchen sollen, Brookes Argumentation zu entkräften. Ihr Augenmerk soll insbesondere auf Brookes schweren (und **Ihrer** Ansicht zufolge falschen) Vorwürfen den Briten gegenüber und ihrer Fehlbeurteilung (ebenfalls gesehen aus der Perspektive des Bürgers aus Turnbridge Wells) der politischen Lage in Großbritannien liegen.

Lösungsschritte zu Aufgabe 3.2

1	Prüfen Sie die verwendeten Operatoren und Hinweise. Diese geben Ihnen genaue Informationen darüber, was Sie in der Aufgabe zu leisten haben (hier: *write a letter to the editor*).
2	Scannen Sie den Text und Ihre Aufzeichnungen kurz nach Informationen zu den relevanten Teilaspekten: *Brooke's reproaches to the British public, political situation in the UK.*
3	Es ist wichtig, dass Sie die Perspektive eines großbritannientreuen Kleinstadtbürgers komplett beibehalten.
4	Achten Sie auch bei Ihren Formulierungen darauf, dass sie zum Sprachgebrauch eines erwachsenen politisch interessierten Menschen passen müssen. Beispiel: Verwenden Sie keine *colloquialisms,* sondern behalten Sie ein hohes Sprachniveau bei. Sie möchten in Ihren Aussagen ernst genommen werden.
5	Überprüfen Sie am Ende, ob Sie alle Formelemente zum Verfassen eines Leserbriefs beachtet haben.

Ausführlicher Lösungsvorschlag zu Aufgabe 3.2

Sir,

I read the article “Has anybody in Britain actually read ‘1984’?”(13 October 2005) with great interest. Still I feel that Brooke’s reproach to the British is a little exaggerated.

We do not live in a Big Brother society. The surveillance that is admittedly more present than before 7 July 2005 (bomb attacks in London) is merely an attempt to insure the citizens’ security and not to cut down personal freedom.

In today’s globalized society crime is not so easily fought with old-fashioned forms of interrogation et cetera. Criminals operate on an international level, they use the Internet to connect

with each other so we have not only the “British criminals” to deal with but gangs from all around the world. Camera surveillance and the possibility of accessing to the personal data of suspects are a great help in fighting international crime.
We want to feel secure again and seeing the means that are being taken to protect us makes us feel safer.
I have to disagree with Brooke’s statement that the British have a “lamb-like disposition toward [their] leaders”. Silence can be a form of approval - it is not always a sign of being unpolitical or uninterested.
We are not all addicts to the “junk diet of celebrity piffle”. I consider it a pity that Brooke stoops to using trivial statements and reproaches to get her message across. It weakens her credibility when she ironically adds the possibility of “armed violence” to the list of possible and acceptable reactions to the camera surveillance in British buses.
She has a point in warning us that the increase of surveillance might have serious consequences. We have to be aware that nothing provides 100% protection against (terrorist) attacks. We have to be careful about our personal data. This also means that we should not thoughtlessly publish our most private affairs in online communities like Facebook. We, the British - and that includes the government and the police of course as well - have a responsibility to our country. We need to make it as safe as possible for future generations.
The price that has to be paid is to my mind worth every single penny.

Peter York
Turnbridge Wells

(365 words)

Schnell-Check zu Aufgabe II

Aufgabe	Thema/ Aufgabentyp			Trainingstipps
1	*Outline ...* Eine im Text dargestellte Sichtweise umreißen			■ Üben Sie, einen Text nach relevanten Informationen zu scannen. ■ Wiederholen Sie die Kriterien zum Verfassen einer *summary*. ■ Schlagen Sie themenrelevantes Vokabular nach, um sich sprachlich vorzubereiten. ■ Wiederholen Sie Konnektoren, um Ihren Text logisch zu strukturieren.
2	*Examine ...* Einen Sachverhalt untersuchen			■ Wiederholen Sie das entsprechende Fachvokabular für folgende Bereiche: *structure* und *language*. ■ Üben Sie Formulierungen, in denen Sie z. B. die Argumentationsstruktur eines Textes beschreiben, die verschiedenen Argumente benennen, die sprachliche Umsetzung analysieren und die Wirkung auf den Leser erläutern. ■ Wiederholen Sie die Kriterien zum Verfassen eines Essays. ■ Üben Sie das Formulieren von *paragraphs*.
3.1	*Discuss ...* Eine Aussage aus dem Text kritisch erörtern			■ Sehen Sie Ihre Unterlagen durch und erstellen Sie Begriffsnetze oder Mindmaps, um Ihr Wissen und Ihren Lernstoff zu vernetzen. ■ Üben Sie, die verschiedenen Einzelbereiche in einer sinnvollen Reihenfolge zu verknüpfen, sodass die einzelnen *paragraphs* sachlogisch aufeinander aufbauen. ■ Wiederholen Sie die Kriterien zum Verfassen eines Essays. ■ Schlagen Sie themenrelevantes Vokabular nach, um sich sprachlich vorzubereiten.
3.2	*Write a letter to the editor ...* Einen Leserbrief schreiben			■ Üben Sie, Leserbriefe zu verfassen. Wiederholen Sie die Formelemente und den typischen Aufbau. ■ Üben Sie, die in der Aufgabe geforderte Perspektive beizubehalten und das dazu passende Sprachniveau zu verwenden.

PRÜFUNGSAUFGABEN 2010

Aufgabentyp	Textaufgabe: comprehension, analysis, evaluation
Thema/ Schwerpunkt	Utopia and dystopia – exploring alternative worlds: Science and ethics: genetic engineering
Material	Edward Albee: Who's Afraid of Virginia Wolf?
Textsorte	Literarischer Text: Auszug aus einem Drama

Aufgabe I

Aufgabenstellung:

1 Summarize George's account of the "experiment" (l. 39). Focus on the changes envisaged, the potential consequences and different reactions to it. **(Comprehension) (16 Punkte)**

2 Analyse the communication and relationship between the characters. Pay attention to language, stylistic devices and stage directions. **(Analysis) (24 Punkte)**

3 Choose <u>one</u> of the following tasks:

3.1 George finds Nick and his programme of genetic engineering "terrifying" (l. 1). Comment on this view against the background of work done in class. **(Evaluation: comment) (20 Punkte)**

3.2 Nick realizes that he cannot win the argument about genetic engineering at two o'clock on a Sunday morning. Everybody is too tired and drunk. So he decides to call George late on Sunday afternoon to present his case. Write their dialogue. **(Evaluation: re-creation of text) (20 Punkte)**

Text

Edward Albee: Who's Afraid of Virginia Woolf?

The characters are: George, 46, professor of history at an American college; his wife Martha, 52; Nick, 30, professor of biology at the same college; his wife Honey, 26. The scene is George and Martha's living-room. Having met the younger couple at an official university party earlier, Martha has invited them over for a drink. The two couples keep on socializing, talking and drinking through the night.

MARTHA *(to NICK)*: Georgie-boy, here, says you're terrifying. Why are you terrifying?
NICK *(with a small smile)*: I didn't know I was.

HONEY *(a little thickly)*: It's because of your chromosomes, dear.

NICK: Oh, the chromosome business. ...

MARTHA *(to NICK)*: What's all this about chromosomes?

NICK: Well, chromosomes are ...

MARTHA: I know what chromosomes are, sweetie, I love 'em.

NICK: Oh. ... Well, then.

GEORGE: Martha eats them ... for breakfast ... she sprinkles them on her cereal. *(To* MARTHA, *now)* It's very simple, Martha, this young man is working on a system whereby chromosomes can be altered ... well not all by himself - he probably has one or two co-conspirators - the genetic make-up of a sperm cell changed, reordered ... *to* order, actually ... for hair and eye colour, stature, potency ... I imagine ... hairiness, features, health ... and *mind.* Most important ... Mind. All imbalances will be corrected, sifted out ... propensity for various diseases will be gone, longevity assured. We will have a race of men ... test-tube-bred ... incubator-born ... superb and sublime.

MARTHA *(impressed)*: Hunh!

HONEY: How exciting!

GEORGE: *But!* Everyone will tend to be rather the same ... Alike. Everyone ... and I'm sure I'm not wrong here ... will tend to look like this young man *here.*

MARTHA: *That's* not a bad idea.

NICK *(impatient)*: All right, now. ...

GEORGE: It will, on the surface of it, be all rather pretty ... quite jolly. But of course there will be a dank side to it, too. A certain amount of regulation will be necessary ... uh ... for the experiment to succeed. A certain number of sperm tubes will have to be cut.

MARTHA: Hunh! ...

GEORGE: Millions upon millions of them ... millions of tiny little slicing operations that will leave just the smallest scar, on the underside of the scrotum *(*MARTHA *laughs.)* but which will assure the sterility of the imperfect ... the ugly, the stupid ... the ... unfit.

NICK *(grimly)*: Now look ...!

GEORGE: ... with this, we will have, in time, a race of glorious men.

MARTHA: Hunh!

GEORGE: I suspect we will not have much music, much painting, but we will have a civilization of men, smooth, blond, and right at the middleweight limit.

MARTHA: Awww. ...

GEORGE: ... a race of scientists and mathematicians, each dedicated to and working for the greater glory of the super-civilization.

MARTHA: Goody.

GEORGE: There will be a certain ... loss of liberty, I imagine, as a result of this experiment ... but diversity will no longer be the goal. Cultures and races will eventually vanish ... the ants will take over the world.

NICK: Are you finished?

GEORGE *(ignoring him)*: And I, naturally, am rather opposed to all this. History, which is my field ... history, of which I am one of the most famous bogs ...

MARTHA: Ha, ha, HA!

GEORGE: ... will lose its glorious variety and unpredictability. I, and with me the ... the surprise, the multiplexity, the sea-changing rhythm of ... history, will be eliminated. There will be order and constancy ... and I am unalterably opposed to it. I will not give up Berlin!

MARTHA: You'll give up Berlin, sweetheart. You going to defend it with your paunch?

HONEY: I don't see what Berlin has to *do* with anything.

GEORGE: There is a saloon in West Berlin where the bar stools are five feet high. And the earth ... the floor ... is ... so ... far ... below you. I will not give up things like that. No ... I won't. I will fight you, young man ... one hand on my scrotum, to be sure ... but with my free hand I will battle you to the death.

MARTHA *(mocking, laughing)*: Bravo!

NICK *(to* GEORGE*)*: That's right. And I am going to be the wave of the future.

MARTHA: You bet you are, baby.

HONEY *(quite drunk – to* NICK*)*: I don't see why you want to do all those things, dear. You never told me.

NICK *(angry)*: Oh for God's sake!

HONEY *(shocked)*: OH!

GEORGE: The most profound indication of a social malignancy ... no sense of humour. None of the monoliths could take a joke. Read history. I know something about history.

NICK *(to* GEORGE, *trying to make light of it all)*: You ... you don't know much about science, do you?

GEORGE: I know something about history. I know when I'm being threatened.

MARTHA *(salaciously – to* NICK*)*: So, everyone's going to look like you, eh?

NICK: Oh, sure. I'm going to be a personal screwing machine!

MARTHA: Isn't that nice.

771 words

Edward Albee, Who's Afraid of Virginia Woolf? Harmondsworth: Penguin Books, 1965, S. 44–47

Annotations

17 Hunh: expression of approval
24 dank: wet and cold, *here:* disagreeable
28 scrotum: bag of skin containing the testicles
34 middleweight limit: reference to Nick's fitness and the significance of boxing in this play. George once refused to box with his father-in-law. So Martha put on a pair of gloves, approached her husband from behind and knocked him out.
47 multiplexity: complexity, variety
48 Berlin: during the Cold War, West Berlin was a symbol of freedom
49 paunch: fat stomach
63 monolith: a large block of stone, *here:* powerful person or organization that is authoritarian and inflexible
66 salacious: *here*: full of sexual overtones

Aufgabentyp	Textaufgabe: comprehension, analysis, evaluation
Thema/ Schwerpunkt	Shakespeare – a literary 'giant' in the 21st century: Shakespeare and the Elizabethan World In-depth study of a play and corresponding film passages/scenes from theatre performances
Material	Brandon Robshaw: Why it's time to give the Bard the heave ho! In: The Independent
Textsorte	Sach- und Gebrauchstext: Kommentar der internationalen Presse

Aufgabe II

Aufgabenstellung:

1 Summarize the author's views on the importance of Shakespeare today and the conclusions he draws for teaching Shakespeare. **(Comprehension) (16 Punkte)**

2 Analyse the way the author uses structure, argumentative techniques and language to attract and persuade his readers. **(Analysis) (24 Punkte)**

3 Choose one of the following tasks:

3.1 Discuss the author's view on Shakespeare's relevance for young people. Refer to your background knowledge as well as texts by Shakespeare and film adaptations that you know. **(Evaluation: comment) (20 Punkte)**

3.2 Write a letter to the editor of *The Independent* in which you comment on the author's views on teaching Shakespeare. Take into account your own experience of Shakespeare as a German student of English.
(Evaluation: re-creation of text) (20 Punkte)

Text

Brandon Robshaw: Why it's time to give the Bard the heave ho!
The Independent, April 24, 2008

As a tribute to Shakespeare this St George's day, isn't it time we dropped him from the National Curriculum? The Bard is a national monument. Nor is there anything wrong with that. Along with a flag, an anthem and a football team, a national writer is part of the trappings of nationhood. The Italians have Dante, the Germans have Goethe, the French have a pantheon which includes Molière, Racine, Victor Hugo and Proust.

And Shakespeare is peculiarly well-suited to be ours, for both literary and non-literary reasons.

The date of his death and the putative date of his birth neatly fall on our patron saint's day; he belongs to the golden age of Elizabethan expansionism; his history plays chronicle our kings and queens and contain quotable patriotic gobbets ("This precious stone set in the silver sea," "We few, we happy few," etc.). His output is staggeringly prolific - 38 dramatic works in all the genres, several long poems and over 150 sonnets - and his plays work well enough dramatically to be constantly performed today. He had, as George Orwell put it, an amazing skill at putting one word beside another; as well as acute psychological insight, the largeness of mind to give great lines even to minor or unfavoured characters, an unmatched ear for rhythm, and an uncanny ability to coin memorable phrases which, in many cases, have passed into general usage.

One might even say that appreciation of Shakespeare is the touchstone of an educated literary taste. If you don't like him, you don't get it. Voltaire and Tolstoy famously didn't, but then English wasn't their mother tongue.

The trouble is that most schoolchildren today don't like him and don't get it. And this isn't their fault. Shakespeare wrote over 400 years ago. Few people realise how much English has changed in just the last generation. Grammar and vocabulary have altered to the extent that teenagers tend to dismiss anything written before about 1960 as "Old English".

Besides, the large and increasing number of second-language speakers are in the same boat as Voltaire and Tolstoy from the start. We don't have anything like the unified national culture we had when I first studied Shakespeare in the 1970s. Then, most schoolchildren had at least some exposure to the King James Bible, the Book of Common Prayer and Hymns Ancient and Modern. We still didn't find Shakespeare easy, but at least we didn't need to have "thee" and "thou" explained to us.

Even the key selling-point that many Shakespearisms have entered common usage is gradually losing its force as the years go by. I was recently taken aback to discover that virtually none of a class of London teenagers had encountered the expression "one fell swoop". Well, you might say, here's your chance to teach them, then. But that cannot be the justification for making Shakespeare compulsory - to teach outdated idioms that no one under the age of 40 uses.

We need to think more clearly about the purpose of enshrining Shakespeare in this manner. If it's to preserve his national monument status, this is an unnecessary and counterproductive way of going about it. If it is to teach those things that literature is supposed to teach - aesthetic pleasure, understanding of character, moral sensitivity, liberal humanist values, an inkling of the techniques by which literary texts work their magic - then Shakespeare is simply not delivering. It's like handing pupils a treasure in a locked chest. More contemporary texts may not offer quite such riches, but at least the kids could open the box.

Making today's school children read Shakespeare is about as sensible as compelling them to read *Ulysses* or *Tristram Shandy.* For all but a few - the brightest and best-read - it is a form of torture. Yet it's laid down in the National Curriculum that all British children of secondary school age must study not one but two Shakespeare plays. It is, as Will himself would say, a custom more honoured in the breach than in the observance - and in practice, many teachers circumvent the difficulty by teaching a fragment of *Romeo and Juliet* and then showing the class *West Side Story.*

By the time students come to choose their AS-levels, those with a liking for literature should be ready to appreciate the riches Shakespeare has to offer. Let them wait until then. This isn't "dumbing down". Force-feeding children Shakespeare can only induce nausea and a lifelong aversion. If we want Shakespeare to be for all-time as well of an age, we must let students come to him when they are willing and able to make the effort needed to enjoy him. Surely this is a tribute our national writer deserves?

780 words

Brandon Robshaw, Why it's time to give the Bard the heave ho!, in: The Independent, April 24, 2008

Annotations

to give sb. the heave ho: to end a relationship with sb.

1	St George: patron saint of England
9	gobbet: fragment, *here*: piece of literature
12	George Orwell: British author
32	(at) one fell swoop: in one go
43	*Ulysses, Tristram Shandy*: novels by James Joyce and Laurence Sterne
45 - 46	a custom more honoured in the breach: a custom better abandonded than followed (quote from *Hamlet*)
48	*West Side Story*: musical based on *Romeo and Juliet*
49	AS-levels: school subjects chosen at the age of 16

LÖSUNGSVORSCHLAG 2010

Aufgabe I

1 Comprehension: Summarize George's account … Focus on …

HINWEIS In dieser ersten Aufgabe sollen Sie aufzeigen, wie George das „Experiment" aus seiner Sicht darstellt. Beziehen Sie sich dabei insbesondere auf antizipierte Veränderungen, mögliche Konsequenzen und unterschiedliche Reaktionen der Betroffenen darauf.

Lösungsschritte zu Aufgabe 1

1	Prüfen Sie die verwendeten Operatoren. Diese geben Ihnen genaue Informationen darüber, was Sie in der Aufgabe zu leisten haben (hier: *summarize*).
2	Scannen Sie den Text gezielt nach Informationen zu den zu untersuchenden Aspekten *changes envisaged, the potential consequences* und *different reactions to it*. Markieren Sie diese entweder farbig im Text oder notieren Sie sie tabellarisch.
3	Benennen Sie Autor, Titel, Textart und Entstehungsjahr in Ihrem Einleitungssatz.
4	Lösen Sie sich vom Text und formulieren Sie eine kurze Zusammenfassung in eigenen Worten. Denken Sie an die Verwendung des *Simple Present* und von Konnektoren, damit die logischen Zusammenhänge deutlich werden.
5	Vermeiden Sie in diesem Aufgabenbereich Kommentare, persönliche Wertungen oder Analysen.
6	Beachten Sie, dass Sie weder wörtliche Rede noch Zitate verwenden dürfen.
7	Strukturieren Sie Ihren Text in *paragraphs*, welche jeweils nur einen Aspekt beinhalten sollten.

Stichpunktlösung zu Aufgabe 1

George's view of the genetic experiments:

- he illustrates that human nature and society might be changed to a new order and uniformity
- he considers the consequences to be highly alarming; the risks could be among the following: eugenics create a seemingly improved human race, any unwanted genetic features are eliminated; everything is controlled by the state in order to maintain this better version of the world; individuality is replaced by conformity and uniformity supplants diversity
- he also points out that the reactions of people to these changes might differ: while some people might welcome the changes, others like himself are sure to fight against uniformity and loss of individuality
- he expects the new human race to be uniformly beautiful and perfect, the individual to choose professions valuable to the society and the whole society to be stable and without any conflicts
- George mentions two possible groups of people who either favour these changes or strongly oppose them: the scientists' interest in the possibilities of science might lead them to approve of this new world; minorities who do not fulfill the requirements or people who want to keep their individuality are sure to reject this new world order

2 Analysis: Analyse the communication ... Pay attention to ...

HINWEIS Sie sollen in dieser Aufgabe analysieren, wie die einzelnen Charaktere miteinander kommunizieren, und untersuchen, wie ihr Verhältnis zueinander gestaltet ist. Dabei sollen insbesondere *language, stylistic devices* und *stage directions* untersucht werden.

Lösungsschritte zu Aufgabe 2

1	Prüfen Sie die verwendeten Operatoren. Diese geben Ihnen genaue Informationen darüber, was Sie in der Aufgabe zu leisten haben (hier: *analyse*).
2	Scannen Sie den Text und Ihre Aufzeichnungen nach Informationen und Vokabular zu den geforderten Bereichen: *stage directions, stylistic devices (imagery, exaggeration, understatement, personification, rhetorical question, simile, irony ...), language (sentence structure, tone, register, choice of words ...)* und benennen Sie, was Ihnen darüber hinaus noch auffällt.
3	Unterstreichen oder notieren Sie aussagekräftige Beispiele.
4	Formulieren Sie einen Einleitungssatz, in dem Sie thesenartig zusammenfassen, wie sich die Beziehung der Charaktere zueinander (auch: *stage directions*) und ihre Kommunikation (auch: *language, stylistic devices*) gestalten. Dabei wäre es gut, einen funktionellen Zusammenhang zwischen diesen beiden Analysebereichen herzustellen (vgl. Stichpunktlösung - *Introduction*).
5	Erläutern Sie jeweils auch die **Funktion** und **Wirkung** der von Ihnen analysierten Aspekte.
6	Strukturieren Sie Ihren Text in *paragraphs,* welche jeweils nur einen Aspekt beinhalten sollten.
7	Vergessen Sie nicht, am Ende eine zusammenfassende Conclusio zu formulieren.

NÜTZLICHE WENDUNGEN **Stilmittel/stylistic devices**

- choice of words
- sentence structure (ellipse, hypotaxis, subordinate clauses)
- register (e.g. colloquialism)
- irony
- personification
- simile
- rhetorical question
- understatement
- exaggeration
- imagery

NÜTZLICHE WENDUNGEN **Verhältnis der Charaktere/relationship between characters**
- mutual affection vs. aggressive tone and behaviour
- sexually interested vs. sexually uninterested in each other
- dominant partner vs. subordinate partner
- loving vs. detesting each other
- mutual understanding vs. misunderstanding each other's thoughts and intentions
- respect vs. disrespect
- conflicts: generational conflict, relationship conflict

Stichpunktlösung zu Aufgabe 2

Introduction:

- in this scene not only generational conflicts between the two men are displayed but also relationship conflicts between husband and wife on many different levels: this can be concluded from the characters' behaviour (→ stage directions), their partly aggressive choice of words and the usage of stylistic devices to provoke the opponent

Generational conflict/opposing ideologies:

- George involves Nick in a one-sided discussion about the implications of genetic engineering in the course of which he repeatedly affronts the younger man
- George repeatedly addresses Nick as "this young man here", which indicates lack of respect; the reason for acting like this is the fact that George sees in Nick one of those responsible for creating the new and perfect human
- George's degrading and even aggressive choice of words ("conspirator", "ants will take over the world") is supposed to provoke the younger man; he depicts Nick as an immoral and irresponsible scientist
- George illustrates his rejection of this "super-civilization" with its "race of glorious men" by using irony and sarcasm when he talks about chromosomes ("Martha eats them ... for breakfast ... sprinkles them on her cereal"), thus ridiculing his wife and therewith the anonymous masses of uninformed people who agree with everything without understanding the consequences
- he further makes use of positively connoted imagery when talking about his favorite subject "history" which in itself will become obsolete if the dystopian society he imagines becomes real ("sea-changing rhythm ... of history"); he feels "threatened"
- well-placed exaggerations ("the greater glory of the super-civilization") and understatements ("a certain ... loss of liberty", "tiny little slicing operations that will leave just the smallest scar", "all imbalances will be corrected") illustrate the very

real danger that he sees: people will not just lose their freedom, even human reproduction will be controlled by sterilizing those considered unfit to reproduce and all this will be done for the sake of a "better" civilization, a better human race

- Nick's attitude changes in the course of this one-sided conversation, which can be concluded from the stage directions: at first he is slightly amused ("with a small smile"), then he gets angry (" impatient", "grimly", "angry") and in the end he plays along with the unpleasant situation created by George ("trying to make light of it all")

Relationship conflicts:

- the fact that Martha openly shows sexual interest in Nick (stage directions: she speaks "salaciously", statement: "You bet you are, baby.") shows that her marriage to George is not a very happy and fulfilling one; this impression is reinforced by her way of talking to her husband ("Georgie-boy, here"; "You'll give up Berlin, sweetheart. You going to defend it with your paunch?"); she denigrates her husband in front of two relative strangers and even makes moves on the younger man; all of this implies that she does not respect him or care for his feelings
- at the same time George denigrates his wife as well ("Martha eats them ... for breakfast ... sprinkles them on her cereal"), which shows that there are deep underlying conflicts that go beyond the situation shown in the scene
- the marriage of Nick and Honey also shows first signs of a crisis: Honey is so drunk that she has problems following the conversation at all (stage directions: "a little thickly" and her reply: "I don't see what Berlin has to do with anything."), which is also unusual behaviour when meeting people one does not know very well
- Nick can hardly suppress his anger about her ignorance and naivety (stage directions: "angry"; statement: "Oh for God's sake!"), which shows that he is beyond the first stage of love when one finds everything about the other one charming
- her shocked reaction to his outburst (stage directions: "shocked"; statement: "OH!") gives the impression that she did not know before how he really feels

3.1 Comment: George finds ... Comment on this view ...

HINWEIS In dieser Aufgabe sollen Sie zu Georges Statement Stellung beziehen, dass er Nick und seine Arbeit *(genetic engineering)* erschreckend *(terrifying)* findet. Es wird erwartet, dass Sie dabei Ihr Hintergrundwissen einbeziehen.

Lösungsschritte zu Aufgabe 3.1

1	Prüfen Sie die verwendeten Operatoren und Hinweise. Diese geben Ihnen genaue Informationen darüber, was Sie in der Aufgabe zu leisten haben (hier: *comment on*).
2	Scannen Sie den Dramenauszug (Text und Regieanweisungen) und Ihre Aufzeichnungen kurz nach Informationen zu den relevanten Teilaspekten *(genetic engineering)* und überlegen Sie, woran Sie sich zusätzlich aus den durchgeführten Unterrichtsreihen erinnern: *individuality vs. conformity, therapeutic and reproductive cloning, human dignity, personal freedom.*
3	Unterstreichen oder notieren Sie aussagekräftige Passagen.
4	Machen Sie sich Ihre persönliche Einstellung zu diesem Thema deutlich und formulieren Sie diese klar und anschaulich.
5	Formulieren Sie einen Einleitungssatz, in dem Sie eine erste These zu Georges Einstellung zu *genetic engineering* anführen.
6	Bauen Sie Ihren Essay sachlogisch auf und verbinden Sie Ihre Gedankengänge mit passenden Konnektoren.
7	Benennen Sie jeweils passende Belege und Beispiele zur Untermauerung Ihrer Ausführungen.
8	Strukturieren Sie Ihren Text in *paragraphs,* welche jeweils nur einen Aspekt beinhalten sollten.
9	Vergessen Sie nicht, am Ende eine zusammenfassende Conclusio zu formulieren.

NÜTZLICHE WENDUNGEN **Die eigene Meinung ausdrücken/expressing your opinion**

- in my view
- I think
- personally speaking
- to my mind
- one could say
- some people argue that ...
- I totally agree with ...
- I must strongly disagree with ...
- I don't go along with ...
- it might be true that ..., but ...
- it's a fact that ...
- we need to consider ...

Stichpunktlösung zu Aufgabe 3.1

Introduction	■ George's idea of a genetically engineered human race is a nightmarish vision of the future of men. Personally I share some of his apprehensions, because the future he envisions is not so far away today.
Main body	■ George is convinced that the role of music, history, arts and literature will be diminished in favor of scientific progress. Individuality and variety will be replaced by conformity and uniformity, and personal freedom will be cut down by the state to establish a society in which everything and everybody is standardized. ■ What irritates George most is the fact that scientists are working on genetically altering human sperm cells. Thus it might be possible in the future to engineer a supposedly "perfect" human being according to the wishes of the "customers". And today therapeutic cloning is already working on altering genes that cause fatal diseases for human beings. Reproductive cloning helps couples who would otherwise remain childless to have babies. The step of trying to create "designer babies" is not an utterly visionary one anymore. And legal regulations differ from country to country. ■ Admittedly science has not yet progressed far enough to enable scientists to create "super-humans". But the question is already being asked: Should working on embryonic stem cells be forbidden for ethical reasons or is progress an excuse for trying to manage everything possible within human reach?
Conclusion	■ I think it is very difficult to draw a line between the humanistic approach to cure diseases and the scientific approach to create life. ■ For me the creation of a human being should stay within the realms of natural reproduction. I am afraid that if there is the possibility to have "designer babies", George's nightmare of an artificial uniformity of human life might become true in the end. Who does not want the very best for his or her child? The question is: At what cost shall that be achieved?

3.2 Re-creation of text: Nick realizes that ... Write their dialogue.

HINWEIS Nick ist sich darüber im Klaren, dass er eine Diskussion über Gentechnologie um zwei Uhr nachts nicht angemessen führen kann, wenn alle Beteiligten betrunken sind. Sie sollen ein Gespräch entwickeln, das Nick am nächsten Abend telefonisch mit George führt und in dem er seine Beweggründe erläutert.

Lösungsschritte zu Aufgabe 3.2

1	Prüfen Sie die verwendeten Operatoren und Hinweise. Diese geben Ihnen genaue Informationen darüber, was Sie in der Aufgabe zu leisten haben (hier: *Write their dialogue.*).
2	Scannen Sie den Text und Ihre Aufzeichnungen kurz nach Informationen zu den relevanten Teilaspekten: *Nick's attitude towards his job, George's opinion on genetic engineering.*
3	Sie müssen die im Dramenausschnitt dargestellte Perspektive von George aufgreifen und entsprechend der neuen, nüchterneren Situation ausgestalten. Das bedeutet, dass er zwar inhaltlich bei seiner Meinung bleibt, diese jedoch in angemessenerer Form zum Ausdruck bringt.
4	Nick muss sich auf einzelne Aussagen Georges explizit beziehen und diese wertend kommentieren.
5	Die von Ihnen dargestellte Gesprächssituation muss sinnvoll an den Kontext der analysierten Szene anschließen.
6	Achten Sie auch bei Ihren Formulierungen darauf, dass sie zum Sprachgebrauch von Professoren passen müssen. Beispiel: Verwenden Sie soweit möglich die Ihnen geläufigen Fachtermini und bedienen Sie sich insgesamt eines gehobenen Registers.

Ausführlicher Lösungsvorschlag zu Aufgabe 3.2

The next evening Nick phones George to conclude their discussion from the night before.

George: George speaking.

Nick: Hi George. It's me, Nick. I felt like calling you after last night's heated discussion. Actually, I would like to present my view on the topic, because last night I couldn't really get a word in edgewise. And we were all quite drunk, which didn't help my case either.

George: Well, I must admit that I got a bit heated in the discussion. I hope I didn't insult you.

Nick: It wasn't so much your standpoint that insulted me as your choice of words. We are both after all experts in our respective fields. But you were discussing MY field and, frankly, your arguments were based – quite understandably – on fears of the unknown and not on well-founded knowledge about genetic engineering.

George: True. Still, I do hold the belief that there is an actual danger that the manipulation of the human race will have incalculable consequences.

Nick: Working with the human genome is a very dangerous task, which puts a great responsibility upon us. But we do not do it with levity as you suggested last night. You called me a "conspirator", even an "ant" that wishes to take over the world.

George: That was not the point I wanted to make. I am sorry if I tread on your toes.

Nick: I thought you would feel that way, otherwise I would not have called you. You need to see that genetic engineering will do a lot of good: we work on ways to cure cancer, and not on the creation of a "super-human" race. We have very strict regulations, so that any black sheep will not only be stopped immediately, they will be severely punished.

And we do not only work with human genes. Most of the time we try and work on the improvement of crops to feed the hungry in the world. We can make them grow on less water and nourishment, so that they can be cultivated in countries where there is scarcely any good soil. We do research on the breeding of sheep, pigs and cows, again to improve their features for the meat market. We feed the hungry.

George: Nick, I can see that there might be some positive effects of your work. But how can you guarantee that there are no negative side-effects? Will the hungry only be fed and their thirst be stilled? Or will there be other fatal consequences? Do you know what your genetically engineered organisms will do to the normal human organism? Will there be interbreeding? What will happen to the "normal" crops and the "normal" animals?

Nick: This is all at a very early stage. We cannot tell, yet, what the long-term consequences will be. But we are very careful. We supervise everything. If we find out about any negative side-effects, we will stop the program immediately and start anew.

George: Frankly, this is what I was saying last night: There needs to be constant surveillance to keep the unpredictable under control. If it is not yet the improved race of human beings – which are unpredictable – you need to control the mass of scientists and their work. Human nature cannot be controlled. There is bound to be someone who oversteps the border. And that makes me afraid. Nothing you say can convince me otherwise.

Nick: Alright. I just wanted to make my point clear on this subject. And to enlighten you a bit. See you around. Have a nice evening. Bye.

George: Bye and no hard feelings.

(583 words)

Schnell-Check zu Aufgabe I

Aufgabe	Thema/ Aufgabentyp			Trainingstipps
1	*Summarize ...* Einen im Text dargestellten Aspekt zusammenfassen			▪ Üben Sie, einen Text nach relevanten Informationen zu scannen. ▪ Wiederholen Sie die Kriterien zum Verfassen einer *summary*. ▪ Schlagen Sie themenrelevantes Vokabular nach, um sich sprachlich vorzubereiten. ▪ Wiederholen Sie Konnektoren, um Ihren Text logisch zu strukturieren.
2	*Analyse ...* Einen im Text dargestellten Sachverhalt analysieren			▪ Wiederholen Sie das entsprechende Fachvokabular für folgende Bereiche: *stage directions, language* und *stylistic devices.* ▪ Üben Sie Formulierungen, in denen Sie z. B. die Struktur der Kommunikation beschreiben und ihre Wirkung auf den Leser erläutern. ▪ Wiederholen Sie die Kriterien zum Verfassen eines Essays. ▪ Üben Sie das Formulieren von *paragraphs*.
3.1	*Comment on ...* Eine Aussage des Textes kommentieren			▪ Sehen Sie Ihre Unterlagen durch und erstellen Sie Begriffsnetze oder Mindmaps, um Ihr Wissen und Ihren Lernstoff zu vernetzen. ▪ Üben Sie, die verschiedenen Einzelbereiche in einer sinnvollen Reihenfolge zu verknüpfen, sodass die einzelnen *paragraphs* sachlogisch aufeinander aufbauen. ▪ Wiederholen Sie die Kriterien zum Verfassen eines Essays. ▪ Schlagen Sie themenrelevantes Vokabular nach, um sich sprachlich vorzubereiten.
3.2	*Write their dialogue ...* Einen Dialog schreiben			▪ Üben Sie, Dialoge zu verfassen. ▪ Schlagen Sie themenrelevantes Vokabular nach, um sich sprachlich vorzubereiten. ▪ Strukturieren Sie den Gesprächsablauf sinnvoll, lassen Sie die Dialogpartner eine rollengerechte Kommunikation durchführen.

Aufgabe II

1 Comprehension: Summarize the author's views ...

HINWEIS Sie sollen in dieser Aufgabe die Ansicht des Autors über die Bedeutung von Shakespeare (und seinen Werken) in der heutigen Zeit wiedergeben und die Schlussfolgerungen aufführen, die er daraus über Shakespeare (und seine Werke) als Unterrichtsthema zieht.

Lösungsschritte zu Aufgabe 1

1	Prüfen Sie die verwendeten Operatoren. Diese geben Ihnen genaue Informationen darüber, was Sie in der Aufgabe zu leisten haben (hier: *summarize*).
2	Scannen Sie den Text gezielt nach Informationen zu den Themenbereichen *importance of Shakespeare today* und *teaching Shakespeare*. Markieren Sie diese entweder farbig im Text oder notieren Sie sie tabellarisch.
3	Benennen Sie Autor, Titel, Textart und Entstehungsjahr in Ihrem Einleitungssatz.
4	Lösen Sie sich vom Text und formulieren Sie eine kurze Zusammenfassung in eigenen Worten. Denken Sie an die Verwendung des *Simple Present* und von Konnektoren, damit die logischen Zusammenhänge deutlich werden.
6	Vermeiden Sie in diesem Aufgabenbereich Kommentare, persönliche Wertungen oder Analysen.
7	Beachten Sie, dass Sie weder wörtliche Rede noch Zitate verwenden dürfen.
8	Strukturieren Sie Ihren Text in *paragraphs,* welche jeweils nur einen Aspekt beinhalten sollten.

NÜTZLICHE WENDUNGEN **Konnektoren/connectors**

- on the one hand ..., on the other hand ...
- to begin with
- whereas
- instead of
- alternatively
- otherwise
- for instance
- as revealed by
- similarly
- likewise

Stichpunktlösung zu Aufgabe 1

Robshaw's central thesis on the importance of Shakespeare in our time:

- due to the fact that our modern world differs largely from Elizabethan times, Shakespeare should not be part of the National Curriculum any more

Robshaw acknowledges the importance of Shakespeare and his status as a national monument:

- he is a representative of the Elizabethan age
- his history plays contribute to a sense of patriotism
- he has written a multitude of dramatic works and poetry
- his works are of high quality, not only as far as dramatic writing is concerned, but also due to his impressive use of language
- Shakespeare's important influence on the development of the English language

Robshaw puts forward arguments to prove why teaching Shakespeare should not be obligatory anymore:

- there have been further developments in the English language and in the English culture which make it difficult for modern students to understand Shakespeare's work
- a lot of British students are from immigrant families and learn English as their second language; for them it is even more difficult to read and understand Shakespeare
- decoding Shakespeare's work is very difficult for students, which might consequently spoil their joy of reading literature
- in his conclusion Robshaw stresses that reading Shakespeare is an important part of the literary heritage but points out that reading his works should be obligatory only for students possessing the knowledge and skills to thoroughly understand and enjoy this task

2 Analysis: Analyse the way the author uses ...

HINWEIS In der Analyse sollen Sie untersuchen, welche textstrukturellen Merkmale, Argumentationstechniken und sprachlichen Mittel Robshaw verwendet, um seine Leser zu fesseln und zu überzeugen.

Lösungsschritte zu Aufgabe 2

1	Prüfen Sie die verwendeten Operatoren. Diese geben Ihnen genaue Informationen darüber, was Sie in der Aufgabe zu leisten haben (hier: *analyse*).
2	Scannen Sie den Text und Ihre Aufzeichnungen nach Informationen und Vokabular zu den geforderten Bereichen: *line of argumentation, rhetorical devices (e.g. imagery)/ choice of words/register, structure of a text* und benennen Sie, was Ihnen darüber hinaus noch auffällt.
3	Unterstreichen oder notieren Sie aussagekräftige Beispiele.
4	Formulieren Sie einen Einleitungssatz, in dem Sie thesenartig die Meinung Robshaws zum Thema *the role of Shakespeare in teaching modern literature* wiedergeben.
5	Erstellen Sie eine Grobstruktur für Ihren Essay, welche Sie entweder aspektorientiert oder chronologisch an den Textverlauf angelegt gestalten können. Falls Sie sich für eine Gliederung nach inhaltlichen Aspekten entscheiden (vgl. Lösungsvorschlag), umgehen Sie so die ansonsten üblichen Wiederholungen von Punkten, die bereits in vorherigen *paragraphs* genannt wurden.
6	Benennen Sie jeweils **Funktion** und **Wirkung** der von Ihnen aufgeführten Beispiele.
7	Strukturieren Sie Ihren Text insgesamt in *paragraphs,* welche jeweils nur einen Aspekt beinhalten sollten.
8	Vergessen Sie nicht, am Ende eine zusammenfassende Conclusio zu formulieren.

NÜTZLICHE WENDUNGEN **Sprachliche Mittel/stylistic devices**

- choice of words (e.g. provocative, exemplifying)
- sentence structure (ellipse, hypotaxis, subordinate clauses)
- register (e.g. colloquialism)
- irony
- personification
- inclusive we
- rhetorical question
- exaggeration
- imagery (simile, metaphor)
- contrast
- enumeration
- using well-known quotes

Stichpunktlösung zu Aufgabe 2

Argumentative technique	**The author tries to catch his readers' interest:** ■ by choosing a provocative heading that implies that he wants to get rid of England's most famous writer ■ by giving numerous examples, for instance of Shakespeare's suitability as one of England's national monuments (ll. 6–16) ■ by referring back to his own experience with learning about and reading Shakespeare; he points out that it was easier then to study Shakespeare, because schoolchildren were accustomed to the language of the King James Bible, which still bears influences from Shakespearian language ("thou", "thee") **He shows that he is well-read and "knows his Shakespeare":** ■ by inserting many quotes from famous Shakespeare works ("This precious stone set in the silver sea", "We few, we happy few")
Structure of the text	**The text has a clear structure, which enables the reader to follow Robshaw's line of argumentation easily:** ■ introduction to the topic, e.g. presenting the thesis that Shakespeare should not be part of the National Curriculum any more (ll. 1–2) ■ proclaiming an antithesis, e.g. the well-known arguments as to why Shakespeare is a cornerstone of English literature ■ a first conclusion: liking Shakespeare is considered a sign of "an educated literary taste" ■ first counterargument: changes in English grammar and vocabulary make it difficult for English-speaking children to understand and like Shakespeare ■ second counterargument: the cultural diversity and in connection with this the increasing number of people for whom English is a second language are reasons for further difficulties in understanding Shakespeare ■ third counterargument: so-called "Shakespearianisms" gradually lose their status in modern English; a lot of young people do not even recognize expressions like "one fell swoop" ■ thesis: we should not "enshrine" Shakespeare as we are doing now; in order to teach pupils "aesthetic pleasure, understanding of character, moral sensitivity, liberal humanist values, an inkling of the techniques by which literary texts work their magic" we should choose more contemporary and therefore more appropriate works of literature ■ conclusion: to ensure that Shakespeare's works are fully appreciated and understood by students, his texts should only be presented to advanced learners "with a liking for literature"

Choice of words	■ a lot of words and expressions are used that underline Shakespeare's singularity as an author and playwright ("an amazing skill", "largeness of mind", "unmatched ear") ■ personal pronouns and possessive pronouns *(inclusive we)* are used to enable the reader to identify with the author's position ■ the author makes use of different registers, i.e. formal (most of the article, for example: "Shakespeare is particularly well-suited to be ours") and informal English ("give the ... heave ho", "dumbing down"); he addresses Shakespeare informally ("Will") ■ inserting Shakespearianisms like "thee" and "thou" mockingly and ironically implies as well that Shakespeare's language is antiquated
Imagery	■ metaphorically describing "the bard" as a "national monument" glorifies Shakespeare's role in literature and at the same time "enshrines" (→ metaphor) him in a state that thwarts any attempt at modernization ■ forcing ("force-feeding") students to read Shakespeare today is metaphorically described as "a form of torture" ■ similes such as "it's like handing pupils a treasure in a locked chest" again underline the difficulties students have to face when dealing with Shakespeare
Other stylistic devices	■ the author uses rhetorical questions ("isn't it time we dropped him from the National Curriculum?", "Surely this is a tribute our national writer deserves?") to structure his argumentation (beginning and ending) and to personally address the readers and to guide them in the process of making up their minds ■ contrasts (for example: "We still didn't find Shakespeare easy, but at least we didn't need to have 'thee' and 'thou' explained to us") are used to illustrate the contradictions in the modern reception of Shakespeare ■ enumerations underline not only the credibility of the author but also show through numerous examples the quality of Shakespeare's work (ll. 6 – 12) and the lessons that cannot be learned any more by dealing with Shakespearean literature alone (ll. 37 – 41)

3.1 Comment: Discuss the author's view on Shakespeare's … Refer to …

HINWEIS In diesem Essay sollen Sie sich kritisch mit dem Standpunkt des Autors zur Relevanz Shakespeares für junge Menschen auseinandersetzen. Dabei müssen Sie sich sowohl auf den Standpunkt von Robshaw im Allgemeinen als auch auf Ihr Hintergrundwissen und weitere Ihnen geläufige Shakespeare-Texte und Filmadaptionen beziehen.

Lösungsschritte zu Aufgabe 3.1

1	Prüfen Sie die verwendeten Operatoren und Hinweise. Diese geben Ihnen genaue Informationen darüber, was Sie in der Aufgabe zu leisten haben (hier: *discuss*).
2	Scannen Sie den Text und Ihre Aufzeichnungen kurz nach Informationen zu den relevanten Teilaspekten (Bezugspunkte zu *Shakespeare's work, Shakespeare's world, film adaptations of Shakespeare's work*) und überlegen Sie, woran Sie sich zusätzlich aus den durchgeführten Unterrichtsreihen erinnern.
3	Unterstreichen oder notieren Sie aussagekräftige Passagen.
4	Machen Sie sich Ihre persönliche Einstellung zu diesem Thema deutlich und formulieren Sie diese klar und anschaulich.
5	Formulieren Sie einen Einleitungssatz, in dem Sie eine erste These zu Robshaws Einstellung zu *Shakespeare's relevance for young people* anführen.
6	Bauen Sie Ihren Essay sachlogisch auf und verbinden Sie Ihre Gedankengänge mit passenden Konnektoren.
7	Benennen Sie jeweils passende Belege und Beispiele zur Untermauerung Ihrer Ausführungen.
8	Strukturieren Sie Ihren Text in *paragraphs,* welche jeweils nur einen Aspekt beinhalten sollten.
9	Vergessen Sie nicht, am Ende eine zusammenfassende Conclusio zu formulieren.

Stichpunktlösung zu Aufgabe 3.1

Introduction:

- As Robshaw discusses in detail in his article "Why it's time to give the Bard the heave ho!" there is a wide gap between the role of Shakespeare as a national monument of English literature on the one hand and his incomprehensibility for modern students on the other hand. Robshaw demands that reading Shakespeare should not be completely omitted from the curriculum, but that it should remain part of the literary education only of advanced students.

Main body:

- This can be seen critically: How can the status of the artist be maintained if students are no longer familiar with his works?
- There are a multitude of arguments in favor of keeping Shakespeare on the National Curriculum besides those mentioned in the article like his "amazing skill at putting one word beside another", the "acute psychological insight, the largeness of mind to give great lines even to minor or unfavoured characters", his "unmatched ear for rhythm and an uncanny ability to coin memorable phrases which, in many cases, have passed into general usage".
- The characters and conflicts portrayed are timeless, for example the tragedy of love unfulfilled *(Romeo and Juliet)*, the comedy depicting stereotypical ideas of manhood and womanhood *(The Taming of the Shrew)*.
- Readers get the opportunity to question their own beliefs and value systems and compare them to those depicted in Shakespeare's works (Should a life without fulfilled love be ended or is this a sin? cf. *Romeo and Juliet*), i.e. the Elizabethan view of the world and of humanity (Is the order of the macrocosm reflected in the microcosm?), which entails a broadening of the horizons of the readers.
- At the same time Robshaw clearly states the problems modern readers have to face when dealing with Shakespeare: The language and the topics are not easily accessible for our schoolchildren. They are not brought up with the King James Bible anymore and therefore have serious problems trying to understand Shakespeare's language.
- To really understand the topics dealt with in Shakespeare's work one must also study the complicated Elizabethan system of values and beliefs. Otherwise the complexity of his works cannot be appreciated.
- Personally speaking I did not at once see the elements of comedy in many of the scenes of *Romeo and Juliet* which we read in class. Only watching *Shakespeare in Love* and the Baz Luhrman adaptation of *Romeo and Juliet* helped me understand not only the historical setting of the plot *(Shakespeare in Love)* but also the dramatic staging and development of the conflict that leads to the death of the two lovers. Just reading the play and secondary texts on Elizabethan times would not have enabled me to fully appreciate the images created and the language used *(Romeo and Juliet)*.

Possible conclusion:

- Reconsidering the arguments in favour of and those against keeping Shakespeare on the National Curriculum, I must say that any student of English should at least be acquainted with the content of some of Shakespeare's works. There are certainly some that are easier to understand than others. But they could very well be translated into modern English. To appreciate the language of Shakespeare, I think, one must be an advanced student. In this point I fully agree with Robshaw. But why should the others be denied exposure to important works of literature? There are numerous good film adaptations of Shakespeare's plays that can be watched and discussed and beautiful sonnets to be read.

3.2 Re-creation of text: Write a letter to the editor ... Take into account ...

HINWEIS In dieser Aufgabe sollen Sie aus Ihrer Perspektive als deutscher Lerner der englischen Sprache einen Leserbrief an *The Independent* verfassen, in welchem Sie Stellung zu Robshaws Aussagen über Shakespeare als Unterrichtsgegenstand beziehen.

Lösungsschritte zu Aufgabe 3.2

1	Prüfen Sie die verwendeten Operatoren und Hinweise. Diese geben Ihnen genaue Informationen darüber, was Sie in der Aufgabe zu leisten haben (hier: *write a letter to the editor*).
2	Scannen Sie den Text und Ihre Aufzeichnungen kurz nach Informationen zu dem relevanten Aspekt: *teaching Shakespeare.*
3	Es ist wichtig, dass Sie Ihre besondere Perspektive als Fremdsprachenlerner(in) verdeutlichen und diese komplett beibehalten.
4	Achten Sie auch bei Ihren Formulierungen darauf, dass sie zum Sprachgebrauch eines erwachsenen, politisch und gesellschaftlich interessierten Menschen passen müssen. Beispiel: Verwenden Sie keine *colloquialisms,* sondern behalten Sie ein hohes Sprachniveau bei. Sie möchten in Ihren Aussagen ernst genommen werden.
5	Überprüfen Sie am Ende, ob Sie alle Formelemente zum Verfassen eines Leserbriefs beachtet haben.

Ausführlicher Lösungsvorschlag zu Aufgabe 3.2

Sir,

I read the article "Why it's time to give the Bard the heave ho!" (24 April 2008) with great interest.

And I must say that I fully agree with Robshaw's demand to have only advanced students of English study Shakespeare's works in depth and not force all students to read two plays by Shakespeare.

For me as a German student of English studying Shakespeare was at first something I was afraid to start. I was afraid of the difficulty of this task, although I am an advanced student of English. But after getting to know certain aspects of the Shakespearian language and learning about the Elizabethan value system and beliefs, reading *Romeo and Juliet* became not only interesting but entertaining. Shakespeare does deal with topics that are now – as they were then – modern and interesting: opposing sets of values in two different families, the question whether fate or human decisions dictate the course of events (of course Shakespeare's view on this might differ from my personal one) or simply portraying teenage lovers with all their overwhelming emotions.
It is surely easier to read contemporary writers, even though their works are challenging on a different level. But still: reading a play by this "literary giant" and making sense of it gave me a feeling of personal success. I set myself a difficult task and succeeded.
Watching Baz Luhrman's modern adaptation and listening to Shakespeare's lines provided an even deeper understanding of possible parallels between our modern world and the Elizabethan setting. And again: I was proud to be able to understand a literary masterpiece.
Admittedly there are obstacles for all students of English, in Germany as well as in the UK: In both countries the number of people with English or in my country German as second language is steadily increasing. As Robshaw said in his article: The command of the language spoken in England (and also in Germany) is decreasing. And this is not only a problem of second-language speakers but also of native speakers. English and German are becoming more simplified with the result that the rather complex language of Shakespeare becomes more and more difficult to understand.
But this should not be an excuse to ban Shakespeare from the National Curriculum in the UK or from the "zentrale Abiturvorgaben" in Germany.
There are ways to enable all students of English to deal at least at some level with Shakespeare. Take the numerous good film adaptations, some beautiful sonnets or even modernized versions of Shakespeare's plays. The "message" of Shakespeare, or parts of it, can be conveyed through any of these. There are always different levels of understanding, so why should the enjoyment of Shakespeare be denied?

Sandra Weller
Cologne

(452 words)

Schnell-Check zu Aufgabe II

Auf-gabe	Thema/ Aufgabentyp			Trainingstipps
1	*Summarize....* Eine im Text dargestellte Sichtweise umreißen			■ Üben Sie, einen Text nach relevanten Informationen zu scannen. ■ Wiederholen Sie die Kriterien zum Verfassen einer *summary*. ■ Schlagen Sie themenrelevantes Vokabular nach, um sich sprachlich vorzubereiten. ■ Wiederholen Sie Konnektoren, um Ihren Text logisch zu strukturieren.
2	*Analyse ...* Einen Sachverhalt untersuchen			■ Wiederholen Sie das entsprechende Fachvokabular für folgende Bereiche: *structure, argumentative techniques* und *language*. ■ Üben Sie Formulierungen, in denen Sie z. B. die Argumentationsstruktur eines Textes beschreiben, die verschiedenen Argumente benennen, die sprachliche Umsetzung analysieren und die Wirkung auf den Leser erläutern. ■ Wiederholen Sie die Kriterien zum Verfassen eines Essays. ■ Üben Sie das Formulieren von *paragraphs*.
3.1	*Discuss ...* Eine Aussage aus dem Text kritisch erörtern			■ Sehen Sie Ihre Unterlagen durch und erstellen Sie Begriffsnetze oder Mindmaps, um Ihr Wissen und Ihren Lernstoff zu vernetzen. ■ Üben Sie, die verschiedenen Einzelbereiche in einer sinnvollen Reihenfolge zu verknüpfen, sodass die einzelnen *paragraphs* sachlogisch aufeinander aufbauen. ■ Wiederholen Sie die Kriterien zum Verfassen eines Essays. ■ Schlagen Sie themenrelevantes Vokabular nach, um sich sprachlich vorzubereiten.
3.2	*Write a letter to the editor ...* Einen Leserbrief schreiben			■ Üben Sie, Leserbriefe zu verfassen. Wiederholen Sie die Formelemente und den typischen Aufbau. ■ Üben Sie, die in der Aufgabe geforderte Perspektive beizubehalten und das dazu passende Sprachniveau zu verwenden.